Historical American Biographies

# PAUL REVERE

## Rider for the Revolution

Barbara Ford

**Enslow Publishers, Inc.**

40 Industrial Road          PO Box 38
Box 398                     Aldershot
Berkeley Heights, NJ 07922  Hants GU12 6BP
USA                         UK

http://www.enslow.com

Copyright © 1997 by Barbara Ford

**Library of Congress Cataloging-in-Publication Data**

Ford, Barbara, 1934-
     Paul Revere : rider for the Revolution / Barbara Ford.
         p.  cm. — (Historical American biographies)
     Includes bibliographical references and index.
     Summary: Describes the life of the silversmith who made the
historic ride to announce the coming of British troops to Massachusetts
at the beginning of the Revolutionary War.
     ISBN 0-89490-779-4
     1. Revere, Paul, 1735-1818—Juvenile literature. 2. Statesmen—
Massachusetts—Biography—Juvenile literature. 3. Massachusetts—
Biography—Juvenile literature. 4. Massachusetts— History—Revolution,
1775-1783—Juvenile literature. [1. Revere, Paul, 1735-1818. 2. United
States—History—Revolution, 1775-1783— Biography. 3. Silversmiths.]
     I. Title. II. Series.
     F69.R43F68 1997
     974.4'03—dc20
                                                              96-8828
                                                                CIP
                                                                 AC
Printed in the United States of America

10 9 8 7 6 5 4 3

**Illustration Credits:** Courtesy, American Antiquarian Society, pp. 29, 49,
53, 79; Courtesy of the Boston Public Library, Print Department, p. 105;
Gary Koellhoffer, p. 61; The Greater Boston Convention & Visitors
Bureau, Inc., p. 4; Library of Congress, pp. 28, 69, 101; Courtesy, Museum
of Fine Arts, Boston, p. 40; *Old Landmarks and Historic Personages of
Boston*, Samuel Adams Drake, Little Brown & Co., 1906, pp. 20, 55, 100;
Courtesy, Paul Revere Memorial Association, p. 112, 118; Courtesy, Paul
Revere Memorial Association Photo © Jim Smalley, p. 32; Courtesy, Paul
Revere Memorial Association, Photo, John Miller Documents, p. 76;
*Pictorial Field Book of the Revolution*, B.J. Lossing, Vol. I, Harper and
Brothers, 1850, pp. 11, 74; Stephen Klimek, p. 13; Courtesy, United
States Navy, p.111.

**Cover Illustrations:** New Jersey State Park Service/Stone (background);
Courtesy, Museum of Fine Arts, Boston (inset).

# CONTENTS

*A statue of Paul Revere on a horse now stands in North Boston. In back of the statue is the steeple of Christ Church, also known as the Old North Church.*

| 1 |
|:-:|

# THE RIDE TO LEXINGTON

A little before eleven o'clock on the night of April 18, 1775, a small rowboat pulled up to the ferry dock in Charlestown, Massachusetts. Three men climbed onto the dock. One was Paul Revere, age forty, of Boston, just across the river from Charlestown. He wore a long coat and high boots with spurs—the clothes men wore horseback riding in the eighteenth century.[1]

Revere, a silversmith, was ready to ride to spread the word that British troops were marching from Boston that night.

A small group of men was waiting for him. They talked in excited whispers. The Charlestown men had seen the two lanterns Revere had placed in the tower of Christ Church in Boston. They knew what the signal meant. The Regulars, as the British troops were called, were moving out by water, bound for some destination in Massachusetts. The men in Charlestown had borrowed a horse Paul Revere could ride to warn colonists.

But what was the destination of the troops? And what was their mission?

Lexington and Concord, Revere informed them. The British planned to arrest Samuel Adams and John Hancock in Lexington. The two men had just been appointed delegates to the Second Continental Congress, the organization that represented the thirteen colonies in their disputes with Britain. After Lexington, the troops would move on to Concord to destroy military supplies belonging to the colony that were stored there.

One of the men who met Revere had been on the road to Lexington that evening. The road was patrolled by Regulars, he warned.

The group stopped at a barn owned by John Larkin, a member of the Whigs, the same political party as Revere's. Revere and Larkin also belonged to the same church, the Congregational Church. It was Larkin's horse, already saddled, that was led out of the barn. Revere, an experienced horseman, sized the animal up quickly. It was big and looked strong. The Charlestown men assured him that the horse was one of the fastest in town.

Revere took the reins, put his boot in the stirrup, and swung himself up. A few more words and he was on his way.

Later he would write: "I set off upon a very good horse. It was then about 11 o'clock, and very pleasant."[2]

## The Road to Lexington

Lexington is twelve miles west of Charlestown. After passing through an area called Charlestown Neck, Revere came to the Lexington Road. It was a dirt road, like all roads outside of towns in the eighteenth century. As he had noted, the night was very pleasant—the moon was up and the temperature was mild. Revere kicked his horse into the rolling rhythm of a canter.

Almost at once, however, he saw the horse's head go up and ears go forward. At this late hour, someone was ahead of them on the road. He searched the dark road with his eyes. Two horsemen waited beneath a huge tree beside the road. A few steps further and Revere could see the outlines of what looked like military hats on the men's heads and the bulge of what could be holsters at their hips.

### What Was the Name of Revere's Horse?

Did the horse Paul Revere borrowed from John Larkin of Charlestown have a name? In a genealogy of the Larkin family published in 1930, Brown Beauty is named as a mare that was loaned to Paul Revere for his ride. The mare actually belonged to John's father, Samuel, according to the genealogy.

But Patrick M. Leehey, coordinator of research at the Paul Revere Memorial Association, points out that Paul Revere himself never referred to the horse by name in his accounts of his ride. Also, people in the eighteenth century usually did not name their horses. When Leehey checked records for the estate of John Larkin, he found that Larkin had one horse, which he did not name.

Paul Revere's horse may have been nameless, but as Revere said, it was certainly "a very good horse."[3]

Pulling sharply on the reins, he yanked the horse's head, bringing the horse around before it had even stopped. He dug his spurs into the horse's side. She galloped back up the road they had just come down. Behind him, Revere could hear hoofbeats on the road. Out of the corner of his eye, he saw another horseman riding across the fields. That horseman was obviously trying to cut him off.

Revere's horse was, indeed, fast. The hoofbeats behind him grew fainter. The horse going across the fields was struggling. Revere knew that there were clay bogs in that area. The horse had probably stepped into one of them and gotten stuck.

Still at a gallop, Revere plunged onto the Mystic Road. A native of Boston, Revere had ridden all these roads. The Mystic Road would take him to Lexington in a roundabout way. It was a longer but safer route. At Medford, he stopped for the first time to warn a local militia leader. After that he stopped a number of times to warn residents. At Menotomy (now called Arlington) he turned back onto the road on which he had started.

About an hour after he had started, Paul Revere was in Lexington.

## Revere Delivers His Message

In the window of the Buckman Tavern, a lantern was still burning, showing that food, drink, and lodging were available. Turning onto Bedford Road at the tavern, Revere rode a short distance up the road to the house of the Reverend Joseph Clarke. A Congregational minister, he was a relative of John Hancock. Hancock, Samuel Adams, Hancock's aunt, and Hancock's fiancée were all staying at the Clarke home.

The house was dark, but about eight members of the Lexington militia were keeping guard outside. There was a group of these armed civilians in every New England town. Militias had existed in Massachusetts ever since it had become a colony over a century before. Originally, militias had been set up to protect towns in the many wars and Native American uprisings.

Revere called out to the leader of the militia in a loud voice. The leader ordered him not to make so much noise. People were sleeping.

"Noise!" Revere cried. "You'll have noise enough before long! The Regulars are coming out!"[4] He banged hard on the front door.

Windows flew open all over the house. The reverend looked out an upstairs bedroom window. Hancock and Adams looked out the downstairs parlor window and some of the Clarkes—there were at least ten of them there that night—peered from other windows.[5] Adams and Hancock immediately recognized their fellow activist, Paul Revere, and invited him inside.

The clock inside showed that it was a little past midnight. After Revere had delivered his message, there was no more sleep at the Clarke home that night. A half-hour after Revere's arrival, another horseman appeared. It was William Dawes, who had set out from Boston on a different route to make

sure at least one messenger got through. The two rested for an hour. Then they headed for Concord, six miles away, on their tired horses.

Leaving Lexington, they heard the bell of the Congregational Church. It was summoning militia-men within earshot to Lexington.

As they rode, Revere considered their situation. Both he and Dawes had evaded the British patrols thus far. But what if they were stopped before they reached Concord? Concord would have no warning of what was coming. Suddenly he heard the sound of hoofbeats behind them. But the horseman who overtook them was not a Regular. He introduced himself as Dr. Samuel Prescott, a physician from Concord. He had been visiting his fiancée in Lexington.

When Revere told him about their mission, Dr. Prescott immediately offered his services. Dr. Prescott's offer inspired Revere to

*John Hancock was one of two patriot leaders hiding in Lexington when Paul Revere rode there on April 18, 1775. Revere's warning allowed them to escape from the British.*

develop a plan. He explained his fears about British patrols, telling his companions, "we had better alarm all the inhabitants till we got to Concord."[6] Both agreed. The three riders took turns stopping at each house they passed. They gave the warning and then asked the householders to help spread the news.

## Trouble on the Road

Two miles from Lexington, Dawes and Prescott left their companion on the road while they rode off to alert several farmhouses. As Revere moved forward alone, he saw two horsemen ahead of him, under a tree. Shouting a warning, he swung his horse around. When his friends rejoined him, Revere wanted to attack. "These are two, and we will have them," he said.[7]

The trio rode toward the two horsemen, but two suddenly became four, all in the uniform of the Regulars. They held pistols and swords. Neither Revere nor his companions had arms. One Regular shouted: "Stop! If you go an inch further you are a dead man!"[8]

Ignoring the command, Revere and his friends spurred their horses forward, hoping to force their way through. But the narrow road left little room for maneuvers. The Regulars, waving pistols, forced them into the field next to the road. Prescott

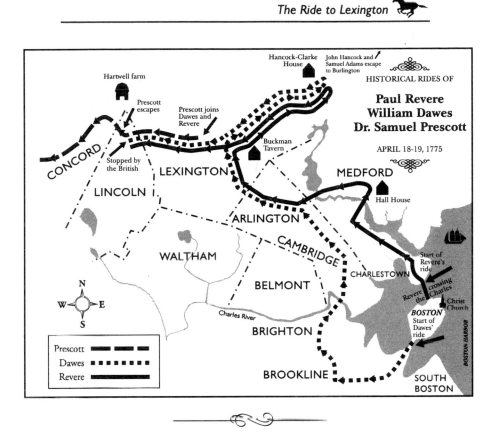

*This map shows the routes that Revere, Dawes, and Prescott took to warn colonists that the British were coming.*

whispered "Put on!" to Revere.[9] The two dug their spurs into their horses' sides. Prescott turned left, jumped a stone wall, and disappeared, followed by several Regulars. Revere turned right and headed for a patch of woods.

Revere's horse must have been tired, but she ran swiftly. Just as she reached the trees, six more horsemen appeared in front of them. Regulars

surrounded the horse and someone tore the reins from Revere's grasp.

When the Regulars chased after Prescott and Revere, William Dawes turned back to the highway. He galloped toward a farmhouse, but his horse pitched him off just as they reached it and dashed away. Dawes limped back toward Lexington. Meanwhile, Prescott's knowledge of the countryside soon put him far ahead of the Regulars chasing him. They returned to the men holding Revere.

Revere was ordered to dismount. "Sir," asked an officer, "may I crave your name?"

"My name is Revere."

"What? Paul Revere!"[10]

The name was obviously well known to these officers. When they turned away to talk among themselves, Revere decided to reveal that he and his friends had alerted the whole countryside. He hoped that would worry them enough to make them forget Hancock and Adams. The two revolutionary leaders were Revere's main concern. When the officers began to question him again, Revere informed them that there would soon be "five hundred militiamen" in Lexington.[11]

Some of the officers hurried away and came back with their commander, Major Edward Mitchell. Revere repeated his story, advising Major Mitchell to leave Lexington as soon as possible.

When Revere had finished, he was ordered to mount his horse again. His reins were taken away. Several other prisoners the Regulars had captured on the road were also put back on their horses. Surrounded by soldiers, they all moved down the highway back toward Lexington—and Boston. A half-mile from Lexington, the party heard a shot. Then there was a whole volley of shots. When the church bell in Lexington began clanging, the Regulars stopped and talked among themselves.

A big British Regular on a small horse was guarding Revere. "Take that man's horse," said an officer, pointing to Revere.[12] The officer ordered Revere and the other prisoners to dismount.

The big Regular climbed onto Revere's horse. The horses belonging to the other prisoners were driven away. Then the Regulars rode off toward Boston at a gallop, leaving their former prisoners standing in the road. It was about three o'clock in the morning. Neither Revere nor the Larkins ever saw the horse Revere had ridden to Lexington again. Later the Larkins were told that the tired mare may have been ridden that night until it died.[13]

## The First Shot of the Revolution

Stumbling over his spurs, which made walking difficult, Revere made his way back to the Reverend Clarke's house. Hancock and Adams were well known for their love of discussion so Revere was not too surprised to find the two still talking in the house. It took until dawn for them to leave. Riding in Hancock's carriage, they set off for the home of another clergyman north of Lexington.

Revere tried to rest at the Reverend Clarke's house. But no sooner had Hancock and Adams gone off than Hancock's clerk appeared at the door. A large trunk belonging to Hancock and stuffed to the top with confidential papers relating to his revolutionary activities had been left at Buckman Tavern. Two men were needed to carry the trunk. Could Revere help? Revere and the clerk walked back to the tavern.

The Buckman, so quiet a few hours before, had been bubbling with activity since Revere's warning. Minutemen, militia members who specialized in quick response to trouble, clustered in and around the building. They explained the shots Revere and the Regulars had heard earlier. There was a law against carrying a loaded gun into a room where drinks were served. So the militiamen fired their guns before they went into the barroom.

Just then a rider galloped up to the tavern door. He shouted that the Regulars were only a half-hour's march away!

Men dashed out of the tavern towards the Green, an open grassy area right across from the tavern. The church bell began to ring. A drummer beat the call to arms. Revere and the clerk hastened up the stairs and located the trunk. Before they lifted it, Revere looked out the second-story window. In the pale early morning light he could see a long line of red-coated men marching down Lexington Road toward the town. Their bayonets gleamed.

But Revere had a job to do. He and the clerk got the heavy trunk down the narrow stairs. Then, heading for the woods, they lugged the trunk through the line of Minutemen who were forming on the Green. Looking back, Revere saw the Regulars moving toward the Green. He and his companion had reached the safety of the woods when Revere heard a shot. He later said that he did not see who fired it.

It was the first shot of the American Revolution.

# 2

# THE TWO PAUL REVERES

A big ship sailed into Boston Harbor early in 1715. It passed Castle Island, a fortified island that guarded the harbor. The passengers aboard the ship, which had come from England, could see Boston's mile-long harbor spread out before them now. In back of the harbor were numerous narrow houses crowded tightly together. Above the houses were the spires of many churches, the tallest structures in the city. Boston, the biggest city in the American colonies, had some sixteen thousand people at that time.

The ship headed for Long Wharf, which extended out into the harbor for some two thousand feet. The largest ships dropped anchor there.

One of the passengers who walked down the ship's gangplank into Boston that day was a thirteen-year-old boy. His name was Apollos Rivoire. His parents lived near Bordeaux in southern France. They were descendants of Huguenots— French Protestants. The Huguenots were being persecuted in France, where they were a minority. Most people in France were Catholic. Apollos's parents had sent him to an uncle on the British Island of Guernsey, probably for both religious and economic reasons. The uncle arranged for the boy to go to Boston, where there were many Protestants.

The uncle may have arranged for Apollos to become an apprentice with a silversmith in Boston. In the eighteenth century, many boys in the American colonies became apprentices to a tradesman such as a silversmith, a carpenter, or a tailor. The boys worked for the tradesman for free, receiving instruction in their trade and room and board in return. When they were twenty-one and had put in seven years as an apprentice, they could open their own shops or work for someone else for a salary.

Apollos was thirteen, the usual age for a boy to become an apprentice. Only the sons of wealthy parents went to school beyond that age. Perhaps that was why Apollos's parents sent him to his uncle at that age. The silversmith to whom young Apollos was apprenticed was John Coney, a sixty-year-old man who was well known for his work in New England. He lived and worked on Anne Street in the section of the city known as the North End.

When he first went to Boston, Apollos probably spoke little English. But before long he adjusted to his new surroundings. Instead of joining the French Protestant Church, he joined the English church to which his master belonged. Like most churches in Boston, it was a Congregational Church. It was called the New Brick Church, or the Cockerel Church.

The name "cockerel" came from the big brass cock, or rooster, that sat on top of the church as a weathervane. The Cockerel was close to John Coney's shop.

*Apollos Rivoire, Paul Revere's father, attended the New Brick Church, nicknamed the Cockerel for the bird on top of the steeple.*

## Apollos Rivoire Makes Changes

John Coney died in 1722, when the apprenticeship of Apollos Rivoire still had three years to run. He was then twenty and, in Coney's papers, he is referred to by a new name: Paul. Paul Rivoire paid the Coney estate forty pounds (the colonists used the English monetary system) for his freedom. In 1729, Paul Rivoire married a young woman named Deborah Hitchborn at the Cockerel Church. The Hitchborn family had lived in the North End for almost a hundred years and owned a small wharf not far from Coney's shop. They had been Paul Rivoire's neighbors.

Just before he got married, Rivoire made another change in his name. Now he called himself Paul Revere.

The year after his marriage, Revere took out an advertisement in a newspaper called the *Weekly News Letter* to inform Bostonians that he had moved. It read: "Paul Revere, Goldsmith is removed from Capt Pitts at the Town Dock to North End over against Col Hutchinson."[1] The new address took the young Reveres deeper into the North End, a city within a city. Mill Creek, which had to be crossed by a bridge, cut it off from the rest of the city. Most residents of the North End had lived there for many years. They stuck together and looked on outsiders with suspicion.

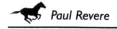 

But Paul Revere was accepted in the North End because he had married into the Hitchborn family. Soon his business was thriving.

The Reveres had a son, John, in 1730, but he died. A daughter, Deborah, born in 1732, was healthy. Then, on December 21, 1734, the Reveres had another son. They named this one Paul after his father. He was baptized at the Cockerel Church like the other Revere children. The family would have nine more children; seven would live to be adults. Big families were the rule in those days, but many children never lived to be adults. Many mothers died young, too. The medical care and drugs we have today were not available then.[2]

### Silversmiths

Apollos Rivoire's master, John Coney, was called a silversmith because most of the work he did was in silver. But silversmiths also did some work in gold. There was not as much demand for gold items as there was for silver because gold was much more expensive than silver. Silver, however, was in short supply in the North American colonies, because silver mines had not yet been discovered there. To obtain silver, a silversmith usually had to melt down coins or an old silver piece that was no longer needed.

When Paul was born, the Revere family was probably living in a rented house at the corner of Love Lane and Middle Street. Boston Harbor, lined with wharves, was only a few blocks away. When young Paul went outside, he could smell salt water and fish and hear the sounds of cargo being loaded or unloaded. If he went down to the nearest wharf, he could walk beneath the long bows of the sailing ships anchored there. The sailors from those ships would be on the streets and in the shops. Boston was an exciting place to grow up.

## Paul Revere Goes to School

But children in the colony of Massachusetts had to study, too. Two laws passed in the mid-1640s required it. One law instructed officials of every township to require that parents and masters of apprentices make sure children under their care could read. Another law required every town with as many as fifty households to hire a teacher to instruct children in reading and writing. This second law made it clear why children should be taught to read. Satan's purpose, the law pointed out, was to keep people from the knowledge of the the Bible. Children had to be taught to read those Scriptures.[3]

Paul probably learned to read in a dame school. This was usually just a room in someone's home. The homeowner, often a woman, was the teacher.

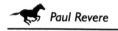 

The word "dame" was a polite eighteenth-century word for a woman.

Many children, including most girls, never went to school beyond the dame school. But once Paul had learned to read, he went to the North Writing School near his home. This was probably when he was seven or eight. There were a number of these public schools in Boston at the time of Paul Revere's childhood. They taught only the basics: reading, writing, and some simple arithmetic. Although the instruction was free, parents had to pay a fee for heating the school during Boston's cold winters. When Paul Revere went to North Writing School, there were about three hundred students. All were boys.

## The Hornbook

Most children in the American colonies learned to read with a hornbook. This was a piece of board shaped like a paddle. A single sheet of text was glued to the board and a transparent sheet of horn placed over the text to protect it.

Horn was a product made from the horns of animals, usually sheep and oxen. The horn was heated until it softened and then it was pressed into a sheet. Horn was also used for lanterns and other items that required a strong, transparent covering.

North Writing School had two floors but no grades. Children learned writing on one floor and reading on the other. On the reading floor, they were called up to the teacher's desk in groups and asked to recite their lesson. The text they used was the *New England Primer*, which had an alphabet and readings from the Bible. On the writing floor, they copied sentences out of the *Primer* with a quill pen. The quills, which were feathers taken from geese, had to be sharpened with a knife.

There was another type of school in colonial Boston too: the Latin School. The sons of Boston's wealthier citizens went to Latin School. At these schools, boys learned not only to read, write, and do arithmetic, they also learned Latin and Greek. They read some of the masterpieces of English literature, too. Boys who graduated from these schools usually went on to a college such as Harvard, which was located in Cambridge, Massachusetts, a town a short distance from Boston.

## An Apprentice Silversmith

By the age of thirteen, when boys became apprentices, they ended their study at the writing schools. It had already been decided where young Paul would spend his apprenticeship—with his father. His shop was in or near the house, and his oldest son had probably been helping him for some

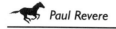 

years.[4] By this time, Paul's father was a well-known silversmith in his adopted town of Boston. Some of the objects he made long ago have been preserved in museums and private collections. Experts say that the silver and gold items he made show a high degree of skill.[5] Paul Revere, Jr., had a good teacher.

The younger Revere did not spend all his time making silver pieces. A document owned by Boston's Christ Church tells us about another of his activities during these years. Erected in 1723 in North Boston, Christ Church had the tallest steeple and finest peal of bells in Boston. But it was an Anglican Church. The Anglicans and Congregationalists, like the Reveres, were both Protestants. But the Congregationalists were the descendents of the Puritans, who had many differences with the Anglicans. The Puritans had founded the Massachusetts Bay Colony a century before.

So Paul's father may not have been too happy when he learned what his oldest son had done. Paul and some of his friends had signed a document that they presented to Christ Church. The document offered their services in ringing the Christ Church bell. The fact that the church kept the document indicates that the boys probably carried out their agreement. For Paul Revere, Jr., and his friends, the chance to climb the tallest steeple in town and ring the famous bell must have been an opportunity they just could not pass up.

Some twenty-five years later, Paul Revere would make use of this same steeple to hang the lanterns that would alert Charlestown.

When the younger Paul Revere was nineteen and his father was fifty-two, Paul Revere, Sr., died suddenly. His wife, Deborah, was left to care for their seven children. Paul Revere, Jr., had been his father's apprentice for six years by then. He was fully capable of taking over. But there was a law that said that to practice a trade, the craftsman had to be at least twenty-one and have had seven years of apprenticeship. Paul Revere was short on both standards. His mother probably ran the business for the next two years.

When Revere was twenty-one, he took a sudden detour in his career. In 1756, he signed up as a volunteer on an expedition that was setting off to capture a French fort at Crown Point on the southern tip of Lake Champlain. The expedition was part of the long struggle known as the French and Indian Wars. The combatants were Great Britain and France, and they were fighting over a big prize—the control of North America. The war was one of many wars that had been going on long before the younger Paul Revere was born. The colonists

*Christ Church's tall steeple had the finest bells in Boston. Paul Revere rang them as a boy.*

were on Britain's side. They thought of themselves as British.

One of the young colonial officers fighting in this war was a Virginian, George Washington. He came to Boston briefly in 1755 to talk with the governor of Massachusetts, William Shirley.

Revere was given a commission as a second lieutenant in the artillery. The artillery consisted of cannons. Perhaps Revere's training in working metal made him handy at repairing these bulky guns, which were made out of brass and copper. At any

*This is a view of Boston as it appeared in 1743, when Paul Revere was a boy. The tallest steeple, on the right, belongs to Christ Church, the "Old North Church." Long Wharf is the structure that juts out into the harbor.*

rate, the pay of an artillery lieutenant was better than that of the ordinary lieutenant. The little army—it consisted of about three thousand men, all of them from Massachusetts—set out for Lake Champlain in the spring of 1756.

They never got that far. Instead, they ended up at Fort William Henry at the northern tip of Lake George. This area is now in New York State. The crowded fort was dirty, and disease soon began killing off the young volunteers. The other danger was the Native American allies of the French. Almost every day, Native Americans picked off men who had been sent off on scouting parties. In November, before the snow fell, the Massachusetts men marched back to Boston. They had accomplished nothing. But at least most of them, like Paul Revere, had survived.

# 3

# A
# SILVERSMITH
# AND MORE

Paul Revere started out with several advantages as a silversmith. Not only had his father been an excellent teacher but he inherited both his father's shop and his equipment. The shop would have had a special furnace, iron blocks called anvils, and various molds and hammers. All of these were used in turning out even the simplest piece of silver.

Since silver was scarce in the colonies, a silversmith first melted coins or old silver pieces in his furnace. But what came out of the furnace was not just silver but a mixture of silver and other metals that had been added to it. The silversmith had to keep melting the silver and removing the other metals until he had pure silver. At that point he added a certain percentage of copper to make the silver hard enough to work with.

Finally, he poured the melted mixture into a mold. When the melted silver hardened into a bar it was called an ingot.

At last, the silversmith was ready to make something out of the silver. He heated the silver, then using a hammer, he pounded the ingot into a thin, flat sheet on the anvil. When the sheet was ready, he put it on another anvil and worked it into a teapot, tray, or other item. During this whole process, the silver hardened as it cooled, so the silversmith had to keep reheating it to make it soft enough to work with. The last part of the process was the decoration.

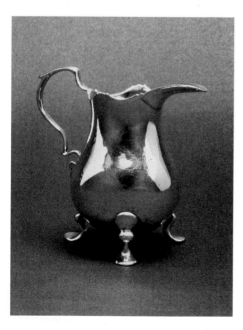

## An Artist of First Rank

Many of the silver pieces that Paul Revere made still exist in

*This cream pitcher is one of Paul Revere's early pieces, made sometime between 1755 and 1765. It would have been used to pour cream into cups filled with tea.*

museums and private collections. Experts who have examined them tell us that Revere was an artist of the first rank. He was able to shape silver into whatever pieces his customers wanted and add different types of decoration. His decoration is particularly good. Sometimes he engraved the outside of the piece, using a special tool. Sometimes he used a hammer to pound a pattern into the inside so that it would be visible on the outside. This is called embossing.

Another way he decorated his work was to use a blunt metal rod to beat a pattern onto a piece. This work was known as chasing and it was difficult to do. Paul Revere did the best chasing work in Boston.[1]

### Paul Revere's Silver

The work for which Paul Revere is best known today is items such as teapots, trays, bowls, and tankards (large covered drinking cups). He made many of these items over the years. He also produced some unusual pieces. One of the most unusual was a sugar dish he made out of an ostrich egg in 1764 for the Oliver family. He also made doctors' instruments and on one occasion, a branding iron.

But at least half of Paul Revere's work was on small items such as buckles, buttons, rings, thimbles, and spurs for use on riding boots.

Making silver objects required a great deal of labor, and Paul Revere did not do all the work himself. His brother Thomas, five years younger than Paul, was his first apprentice. Later there would be other apprentices. New apprentices would sweep the floors for silver scraps, keep the furnace burning, and tend to other menial tasks. Older apprentices would be learning how to hammer and shape the silver. But there was still plenty of work for the master of the shop. In the early years of Paul Revere's shop, he shaped and decorated most of the pieces that bear his mark himself.

Besides making items out of silver and gold, Revere also handled repair work. If someone dropped a teapot and the handle, which was put on separately, came loose, the teapot would come to Revere's shop for repairs. "Mending sundrys," he wrote in his account book during this period, referring to the repair of miscellaneous items. "Taking out bruises," he wrote on another day, referring to the removal of imperfections on a worn item.[2]

In 1757, twenty-two-year-old Paul Revere must have felt confident that his silversmith shop would succeed. On August 17, 1757, he married Sarah Orne. She came from the North End and was twenty-one years old. The couple lived with Paul Revere's mother and his brothers and sisters in their rented house in the North End. Young couples seldom lived on their own then. They could not afford to unless they were quite rich. Soon the house was more crowded than ever: Revere and his wife had a daughter, Deborah, in 1758.

Although Paul Revere was now the master of a busy silversmith shop, he always found time for other activities. In 1760, he joined a group that would be very important to him. It was the Freemasons, or Masons, a men's society that had begun many years before in Britain. Revere's particular lodge, as the individual groups were known, met at the Green Dragon Tavern. Revere was described as a "goldsmith and engraver" when he joined.[3] Another young man joined Revere's lodge at the same time: Joseph Warren, a physician.

Warren was only twenty but he was a graduate of Harvard. He was working for an older physician, doing what would be called an internship today. In spite of differences in education and background, Warren and Revere became good friends.

Paul Revere made other friends at the meetings of the Masons. Soon these Masons were doing business with their new friend. About this time, Revere began keeping records for his shop in a book. One of the first entries notes that he sold a Masonic medal to a member of his lodge. His book also shows that he began to do engravings for notices of Masonic meetings at this time too.[4] Engraving

involves cutting lines into a hard surface. The text or picture that results can be printed. Revere apparently taught himself to engrave.

## Revere Joins Political Clubs

During this same period, Paul Revere joined two political groups, the North Caucus and the Long Room Club. Both were part of the Whig party in Boston. The other party in Boston was known as the Tories. The colonies inherited these party names from Britain. There the Whig party favored a stronger role for the Parliament, the British legislature. The Tories, who were more conservative, wanted the British king to have more power. In the colonies, the Whigs became the party pushing for a stronger role for the colonial government.

Some of the men who joined these two Whig groups in Boston in the 1760s would become famous later. They included Samuel Adams, his cousin John Adams, and John Hancock. Hancock became the wealthiest man in New England in 1764, when he inherited his uncle's fortune.

In the early 1760s, there was plenty for the members of the clubs to discuss. The long French and Indian Wars were finally coming to an end. In 1760, the British had triumphed. All of North America east of the Mississippi River, from Canada to the Gulf of Mexico, now belonged to Britain. The news that Britain planned to station some ten thousand troops in the colonies to keep the peace was almost overlooked in the general good feeling.[5] The colonists, after all, thought of themselves as British. They rejoiced with Britain.

Just as the final battle of the war was won, the old king, George II, died. The new king was George III. At first the colonists felt positive about the monarch who had come to the throne at such a high point in Britain's history.

But the good feeling about George III and Britain did not last. No sooner was the war over than Britain began to enforce old laws that had been overlooked and unenforced before. These laws prohibited trade with France and put other restrictions on colonial shipping. The laws affected port cities like Boston in particular. All during the French and Indian Wars, ships from Boston had gone back and forth to the French-held islands in the West Indies. These islands stretch in an arc from the coast of Florida to South America. There they had traded goods such as beef and leather for island products like molasses. Now this trade was being stopped.

To help them trap smugglers, British officials began using the "Writs of Assistance." These papers allowed them to break into ships, warehouses, and even homes to look for evidence. James Otis, the

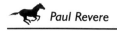 

best lawyer in Boston and a member of the Long Room Club, defended a group of Boston merchants who were protesting the Writs. When the case was heard in 1761, Otis spoke for four hours. He referred to the "rights of man" and called the Writs "instruments of slavery."[6] The speech became famous in Boston. But James Otis lost his case anyway.

## Bad Times in Boston

At the same time that Britain began enforcing these laws, business in Boston began to decline. During the war, Boston merchants and craftsmen like Paul Revere had prospered. The merchants earned money from the illegal trade and from supplying the British troops who filled Boston. The merchants used some of their money to buy goods from craftsmen like Paul Revere. In 1760 and 1761, for instance, Revere made a number of handsome silver trays for well-to-do Bostonians. These trays were given as wedding gifts.

But by the early 1760s, a postwar depression was gripping New England. In Paul Revere's account books for this period, orders for large items are few. The Revere family, meanwhile, was growing. The silversmith and his wife added three more children, Paul, Sarah, and Mary, to their family between 1760 and 1764. In 1765, Paul Revere's goods were seized to enforce payment of a debt for ten pounds. Other craftsmen and merchants were having similar problems. Some went bankrupt.

But somehow, Revere satisfied his debt and the order against his goods was lifted. He rented out part of his shop during this period to save money. This was also when he took up engraving, which would occupy an increasing amount of his time for the next decade. There were no photographs in those days; engravings were the most popular form of illustration. But engravings had many other uses too. Revere engraved just about anything that could be engraved: songbooks; trade cards for businessmen; bookplates; notices; certificates; and illustrations for books, magazines, newspapers, and posters.

Revere did good commercial engravings, such as notices and trade cards. But he copied most of his pictorial engravings and sometimes he did a poor job of it. Nevertheless, engraving did supply some badly needed money to the Revere household.[7]

In the midst of all this, Paul Revere had his portrait painted by John Singleton Copley of Boston. The two men knew each other, as Revere had made metal frames for some of Copley's miniature portraits.[8] The date of the portrait is 1768. Revere probably did not pay for it. A man who had recently had his goods seized for debt was not in a position to pay for portraits. Copley married

*Paul Revere's portrait by John Singleton Copley was probably painted between 1768 and 1770, when Revere was in his mid-thirties.*

## Portrait of a Craftsman

Paul Revere was an unusual subject for John Singleton Copley, who usually painted wealthy merchants and their wives. Copley was the highest paid portraitist in the colonies at this time. Why did he paint Paul Revere? Copley may have wanted to use the Revere portrait for an exhibit of his work. A portrait of a craftsman like Revere would have attracted attention because its subject was unusual. We do know that Copley took great pains with this painting, which is considered one of his best.

There is no record that the portrait ever appeared in an exhibit. By the time the portrait was finished, Revere was becoming known as a patriot. Copley, a British sympathizer, may have been afraid to associate himself publicly with a patriot.[9]

during this period, and Revere might have given the artist some silver pieces for his bride in exchange for the portrait.[10]

In the portrait, Paul Revere wears his working clothes: a linen shirt and a vest. He holds one of the teapots he made in the 1760s. There is a small smile on his lips. He looks like a man who could handle anything that came his way. In the upcoming years, he would need that ability more than ever.

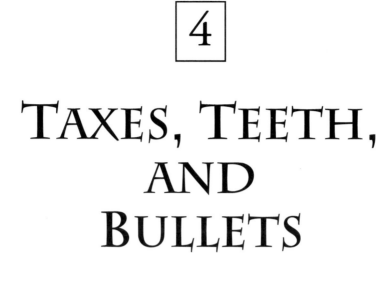

# 4

# TAXES, TEETH, AND BULLETS

In 1765, Britain passed the Stamp Act. This act became famous in American history even though it never actually went into effect. The Stamp Act put a small tax on almost all the paper that was used in the colonies, from legal documents to playing cards. It also required the use of a special kind of paper, which had to be obtained from a special office.

The Stamp Act was a law that irritated anyone who used paper. But it hit merchants and lawyers the hardest, because they used so much paper.

The British Parliament passed this law because Britain, like her colonies, was now in a postwar depression. Britain had won the French and Indian War, but it had been very expensive. British leaders thought the North American colonies, who had done so well during the war, should help pay for it. To Britain's new king, George III, and the Parliament, the Stamp Act was a reasonable measure.

But the colonies did not see it that way. From the Carolinas to Massachusetts, legislators denounced the act. They claimed that only the colonial legislatures—there was one in each colony, with the members elected by voters—could tax the colonists. In Massachusetts, the main spokesperson against the act was Samuel Adams. He was not a member of the legislature but he belonged to the powerful Caucus Club, a political club in Boston.

## The Sons of Liberty

As news of the Stamp Act spread throughout the colonies, secret groups called the "Sons of Liberty" formed to oppose the new law. There was one of these groups in almost every town in the colonies, including Boston. Was Paul Revere a member? Probably, but there is no evidence. In mid-August, the Sons of Liberty hanged a figure of Andrew Oliver on a large elm tree in the middle of Boston.

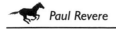 

Oliver was the new stamp master for Boston. From then on the elm was known as the "Liberty Tree."

At dusk on the day Oliver's figure was hanged on the tree, a procession of the Sons of Liberty put the figure on a bier. A bier was what bodies were placed on during funerals. Carrying the bier, the Sons of Liberty marched to the nearby State House. They walked under the windows chanting: "Liberty, Property and no Stamps."[1]

That night, a mob forced its way into Oliver's house. He was not harmed, but the mob broke windows and drank some of his wine. The mob left when Thomas Hutchinson, lieutenant governor of Massachusetts, arrived with a sheriff. A few weeks later, a bigger mob attacked Hutchinson's mansion, which was very close to Paul Revere's house. The yelling of the mob could be heard all over the North End. This time the interior of Hutchinson's house was completely destroyed and the valuables were taken.

Boston was not the only place where the stamp tax resulted in riots. There were disturbances all over the colonies. In the fall of 1765, representatives from most of the colonies held a congress in New York City to discuss the Stamp Act.

Britain realized it had made a mistake. In the winter of 1766, without a penny's tax ever having been collected, the Stamp Act was repealed. The people in the colonies celebrated. In Boston, Paul

Revere probably helped make a huge construction of oiled paper that was set up on Boston Common, a large open space in the middle of the city. Three hundred lamps were placed inside of it. Revere made an engraving of this construction. Bostonians also hung lighted lanterns on the Liberty Tree, which had already become a symbol of the colonies' opposition to British laws.

## A Tax on Tea and Other Goods

But the colonists had celebrated too soon. The very next year, the British Parliament passed the Townshend Acts. They put taxes on a number of goods, including tea. The new taxes set off another round of disturbances. In Massachusetts and some other colonies, people refused to buy British goods. Massachusetts, as usual, was a leader in defying the British. Samuel Adams wrote a letter that the legislature sent to the other colonies. It asked them to resist the new acts.

King George III was so angry when he heard about it that he insisted that the Massachusetts legislators take back their letter.

The legislators refused by a vote of ninety-two to seventeen. The Sons of Liberty in Boston asked Paul Revere to make a special bowl to commemorate the brave ninety-two. He produced a silver punch bowl

big enough to hold almost a gallon of liquid. It became one of his most famous pieces.

He commemorated this event in another way too, with an engraving. It showed the loathsome seventeen who had agreed to take back the letter marching into hell. "A Warm Place—Hell" read the title.[2] From then on, Revere would use his skills in engraving to tell Bostonians about the bad deeds of Britain. Revere was not a good speaker, like his friend Joseph Warren. Revere was not a skillful writer, like John Adams, Samuel Adams's cousin. But through his engravings, Revere was able to deliver political messages.

The Sons of Liberty became active again. In Boston, they slipped out at night with their faces blackened to disguise themselves. In groups as large as a hundred, they surrounded tax collectors' houses, broke windows, and yelled insults. But the more responsible leaders of the Sons of Liberty saw to it that no destruction like that which had been done to the Hutchinson mansion took place again.

The tax collectors and their families were frightened, nevertheless. Most of them moved to Castle Island, a fortified island in Boston Harbor, where a small number of British troops were stationed. Anne Hulton, a relative of one of the collectors, described the nighttime visitors who drove them to Castle Island as the "Sons of

Violence." She lists their activities as "breaking Windows, beating, Stoning & bruizing several gentlemen belong'g to the Customs."[3]

## Britain Sends Troops

The Castle Island refugees requested help from Britain, and in 1768, it arrived. On September 30, 1768, as Anne Hulton watched from Castle Island and Paul Revere watched from the mainland, eight transports and ships of war sailed into Boston Harbor. The onlookers could see the bright red coats of the British Regulars on deck. The next day, Revere and most of Boston saw some six hundred men march off the ships and onto Long Wharf, the longest wharf in Boston.

At the end of the French and Indian War, Britain had announced it would put ten thousand Regulars in the colonies as protection from Native Americans and "foreign aggressors."[4] To Bostonians it looked as if troops were being used to control the colonists.

In his shop, Revere began a new engraving. Based on the artwork of another Bostonian, it shows the British ships arriving at Long Wharf. Under the print, Revere describes the event, using the word "insolent," which means overbearing or arrogant, to convey the way the troops looked as they marched off the dock. He wrote, "there Formed and Marched with insolent Parade, Drums beating, Fifes

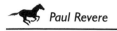
playing, and Colours flying, up King Street. Each Soldier having received 16 rounds of Powder and Ball."[5]

Even though these important events were happening right in front of him, Paul Revere still had to make a living. The Reveres now had five children and the silversmith shop was not receiving many orders. In 1768, Paul Revere added dentistry to his skills. In September, the same month the British Regulars arrived, readers of the *Boston Gazette* found this advertisement in the paper:

> Whereas many persons are so unfortunate as to lose their Fore-Teeth by Accident, and otherways, to their great Detriment, not only in Looks, but speaking both in Public and Private:—This is to inform all such, that they may have them re-placed with artificial Ones, that looks as well as the Natural & answers the End of Speaking to all Intents, by PAUL REVERE, Gold-smith, near the Head of Dr. Clarke's Wharf, Boston.[6]

At the end of the advertisement, Revere explained that he learned dentistry from a visiting "Surgeon-Dentist."[7]

Even though he was busy with his several careers, Revere did not forget about the British Regulars. No resident of Boston could forget them. The main guardhouse was right across from the State House, and soldiers were camped all over town, including Boston Common. Before long, a number of incidents had occurred. Soldiers and civilians fought in taverns. British soldiers were "accidentally" pushed off wharves. Often children followed soldiers shouting "Lobsters!" Lobster was a nickname for the red-coated troops.

## Bullets at the State House

March 5, 1770, was a cold day in Boston. The snow lay a foot deep. In spite of the cold and snow, several hundred men had gathered in front of the State House that evening. They threatened the lone sentry at the guard post across from the State

*Paul Revere made this engraving of British warships anchored in Boston Harbor in 1768. The ships were there in response to the riots connected with the Townshend Acts.*

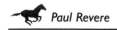 

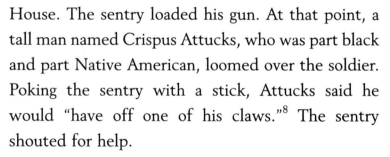

**Paul Revere, Dentist**

The false teeth Paul Revere put in people's mouths were probably made from the tusks and teeth of various animals. Porcelain teeth, like the ones produced today, were not available yet. The teeth were fastened to their natural neighbors with wires. The results were not much use in chewing, but they did help people look and speak better, as Revere's advertisement points out. Nevertheless, many people who lost their teeth did not bother with false ones. An early nineteenth century portrait of Paul Revere's second wife shows that she had missing teeth that had not been replaced.

House. The sentry loaded his gun. At that point, a tall man named Crispus Attucks, who was part black and part Native American, loomed over the soldier. Poking the sentry with a stick, Attucks said he would "have off one of his claws."[8] The sentry shouted for help.

Seven soldiers and Captain Thomas Preston, the officer of the day, ran out of the guard house. Preston ordered his men to load their guns. Suddenly the crowd moved forward toward the soldiers. At the same time, Attucks hit at the sentry with his stick but knocked down another soldier instead. The soldier jumped up, clutching his musket. Above the yells of the crowd, someone was heard shouting "Fire!" The crowd retreated when shots sounded, leaving five men on the snowy ground. One was Attucks.

After the shots were fired, Preston went in front of his men, pushing up their guns to prevent them from firing again. Drums began to beat all over Boston, calling soldiers to arms. The Regulars, each with his gun, lined up in front of the State House. Lieutenant-Governor Hutchinson arrived at the State House. By that time, it was known that four men had been killed and another seriously wounded. The wounded man died a few days later.

Hutchinson made a speech from the balcony of the State House, promising that justice would be done. Captain Preston and his eight men were arrested before dawn and charged with murder.

If Revere was not in the crowd that confronted the soldiers that night, he must have arrived soon afterward. For the trial of the soldiers, someone prepared a pen and ink diagram of the scene, showing where the various participants stood. The handwriting on the diagram looks like Revere's, and it is generally accepted that he did the diagram.

A few days later, Revere went to work on an engraving of the event. It became his best-known

engraving and one of the most famous engravings ever made in this country.

The trial of the soldiers involved in the shooting took place a short time later. They received a fair trial. John Adams was one of the lawyers for the defense. The injured man lived long enough to testify that the crowd had taunted the soldiers and struck one of them. All of the British soldiers were acquitted except two, who were found guilty of manslaughter. They were branded on the thumb. As

### The Boston Massacre Engraving

Paul Revere's engraving was not based on the diagram he is believed to have made right after the event. In the engraving, red-coated soldiers stand in a straight line and fire at a line of civilians. None of the civilians are doing anything to provoke the soldiers. Like most Revere engravings, this one uses the artwork of another person. In this case it was Henry Pelham, a Boston artist and engraver.

Across the top of Revere's engraving are these words: "The Bloody Massacre perpetuated in King Street on March 5, 1770 by a party of the 29th Reg't."[9] From then on, the event was known as the Boston Massacre.

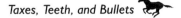

The BLOODY MASSACRE perpetrated in King—ſ—Street BOSTON on March 5th 1770 by a party of the 29th REGt.

BUTCHER'S HALL

Engrav'd Printed & Sold by Paul. REVERE BOSTON

*Paul Revere's engraving of the Boston Massacre became his best-known engraving.*

a result of the Boston Massacre, the British troops were withdrawn from Boston.

On the very day of the Massacre, the British Parliament repealed most of the duties imposed by the Townshend Acts. The only tax left in place was the small one on tea.

# 5

# REVERE'S
# FIRST RIDES

In 1770, Paul Revere was thirty-five years old. At the beginning of the year, he and Sarah and their five children were still living in the same rented house at the head of Clarke's Wharf. But in February, Revere made a big move. He bought his first house, taking out a mortgage of 160 pounds to do it. The house was on North Square in the North End and right in back of the Cockerel Church that the Reveres attended.

The house was almost a hundred years old when the Reveres bought it. Today it still stands in the city of Boston as a memorial to Paul Revere. In his day, there was a large yard behind the house that ran all the way back to the Cockerel. Revere sold part of this yard and built a barn on his own part. Then he bought a horse. He did not need a horse for his business or to go to church or to market. The church was right in back of him and the market in front of him, in North Square.

We do not know why he bought a horse, but whatever his reason, Revere's ability to ride would turn out to be very important in American history.

In March of 1771, Revere's house became the center of a nighttime event. Revere used the house for a memorial to a boy who had been killed by a customs officer and the victims of the Boston Massacre. Every window in the house that faced the street showed an illuminated scene. In one window was the ghost of the boy, trying to stop the flow of his blood. In another scene, the victims of the Boston Massacre lay on the ground with blood running from

*Paul Revere's house (center) in North Square looked like this in the late nineteenth century, before it was restored. It had three stories, as it did when the Reveres lived there.*

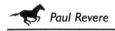 

their wounds. Still another showed a woman, representing America, grinding a British Regular under her foot.

Bostonians crowded North Square to see the display. According to the *Boston Gazette*, "Thousands were struck with Solem Silence & their Contenances covered with a meloncholy [sic] Gloom."[1]

Late in 1772, Sarah Revere had her eighth child. She never recovered from the birth and died in the

**Paul Revere's First House**

The first house Paul Revere owned was built around 1680 by a prosperous merchant. The house was considered very fashionable when it was built, with its second story jutting out over the first, and its casement windows that swung out like doors. When Paul Revere bought the house a hundred years later, however, it was outdated. Revere put on a third story to help house his big family. The Reveres lived in the house until about 1799.

In the nineteenth century, the house was split up into small apartments. The house was in such poor condition by 1905 that it was slated to be pulled down, like other old houses on North Square. The new interest in Paul Revere resulted in the house being acquired by the Paul Revere Memorial Association. The third story was removed, so that the exterior looks much the way it did when it was built. Inside, some of Paul Revere's furniture, silver, and other items reflect the Revere period.

spring of 1773 at the age of thirty-seven. Sarah's last baby died a few months later. Luckily, Revere had his mother to help him care for his other children.

Before long—only five months—he had a new wife. The marriage took place in October of 1773, and the new bride immediately moved into the house on North Square. There were no honeymoons for people like the Reveres in the eighteenth century. The bride's name was Rachel Walker, and she, like Sarah, came from Boston's North End. She was twenty-seven, eleven years younger than Paul Revere. Revere called her "the Fair One that is nearest my Heart" in a poem he wrote to her during their courtship.[2]

## The Problem with Tea

The year of Paul Revere's second marriage would turn out to be an important one for the colonies and especially for Boston. The Townshend Acts had left a small tax on tea. It irritated the colonists, but by 1773, most of them had apparently decided to go along with it. They continued to drink tea, all of which had to be imported from Britain. Tea was grown in Asia and brought to Britain by large firms like the East India Company. But in the middle of 1773, the British Parliament decided to give the East India Company a monopoly on tea in the colonies.

This meant that merchants in Boston who were accustomed to importing tea from Britain and then selling it would not be able to do so. Only the East India Company would be able to import tea. It would also control the price.

In the eighteenth century, tea was very important in the colonies. The colonists did not drink much coffee; their favorite beverage was tea. They drank tea the way people in Britain drank tea and still drink it. In wealthy colonial families, tea-drinking was not only a daily activity but the center of a ceremony. The ceremony involved special tables, silver pieces, and china cups and saucers. Paul Revere made many silver teapots and other pieces for the tea ceremony. The biggest order he ever received for silver was for a tea set.

So when news of the East India Company's monopoly on tea reached the colonies, the people were furious. Bostonians were even more angry when they learned that the sons of Thomas Hutchinson were among the few who would be able to sell tea. Boston merchants like John Hancock were left out. There had been times when Hancock, who was the richest man in New England, had sympathized with Britain. But even he joined with the other colonists in their fury.

In late November 1773, the first of the tea ships arrived in Boston Harbor. All over Boston, signs appeared summoning residents to a meeting at Faneuil Hall. This building was on the Boston side of Mill

Creek, the stream dividing the city from the North End. At this meeting, and one following it, resolutions were passed demanding that the tea ship return home without landing the tea. Meanwhile, two more tea ships arrived. All three anchored at a wharf in the south part of Boston. Hutchinson, who had become the governor of Massachusetts, refused to let any of them leave if they did not land their cargo.

Each night, parties of men watched the ships so that they would not be unloaded. Paul Revere may have been one of these men. After twenty days, according to customs regulations, cargoes could be seized if not landed. If that happened the tea would be brought to shore.

On the night of December 16, 1773, some five thousand people—a third of the population of Boston—gathered at the Old South Meeting House. A messenger had been sent to Hutchinson, who had retreated to a town near Boston, asking him to let the ships leave. At six o'clock, the messenger came back. Hutchinson had refused. When Samuel Adams announced the news, there were shouts throughout the building. Men began hurrying out into the night.

George Hewes, who was there that night, remembered someone shouting, "Let every man do his duty, and be true to his country."[3]

Plans had already been made in the North Caucus for what would be done if Hutchinson refused to let the ships leave. A number of men, probably including Paul Revere, went to a nearby house or possibly the Green Dragon Tavern. The men put on ragged clothing and dabbed red paint and a sooty black substance that came from oil lamps on their faces. Some added blankets. Most carried a hatchet. The idea was that they would look like Native Americans.

Then the men rushed down to the wharf. The wharf and the area around it were full of people. They watched silently as the men divided themselves into three groups, each with a leader. Then each group boarded a ship. One man who wrote about his part in the tea party later related that the mate on the ship he boarded handed over keys and lights without argument. When the heavy wooden tea chests (they weighed about four hundred fifty pounds) were found, the men broke them open with their hatchets and threw the tea into the harbor.

By dawn, 342 chests containing some ten thousand pounds of tea had been dumped. Today, the amount of tea destroyed would be worth about 1.5 million dollars. The men forced one individual, who tried to keep a small amount of tea, to run a

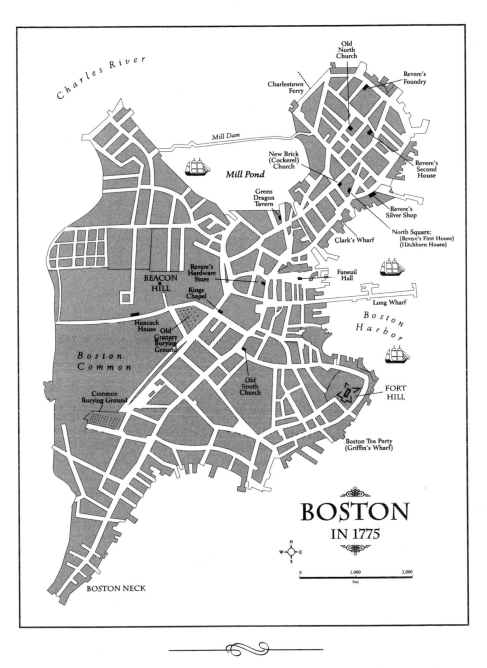

Charles River

Old
North
Church

Charlestown
Ferry

Revere's
Foundry

Mill Dam

New Brick
(Cockerel)
Church

Mill Pond

Revere's
Second
House

Green
Dragon
Tavern

Revere's
Silver Shop

Clark's Wharf

North Square:
(Revere's First House)
(Hitchborn House)

Revere's
Hardware
Store

Faneuil
Hall

BEACON
HILL

Kings
Chapel

Long Wharf

Boston
Harbor

Hancock
House

Old
Granary
Burying
Ground

Boston
Common

FORT
HILL

Common
Burying Ground

Old
South
Church

Boston Tea Party
(Griffin's Wharf)

**BOSTON**
IN 1775

N
W   E
S

0          1,000          2,000
Feet

BOSTON NECK

*This map of Boston in 1775 shows important places for Paul Revere.*

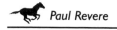 

gauntlet between two lines of men. They struck the man as he ran by.

Paul Revere never admitted to being part of the "Boston Tea Party," as it soon came to be known. But before long, people in Boston were singing a ballad that mentions only two members of the Tea Party, Joseph Warren and Paul Revere. Part of the song goes like this:

> Rally Mohawks! Bring out your axes,
>
> And tell King George we'll pay no taxes
>
> On his foreign tea . . .
>
> Our Warren's there, and bold Revere
>
> With hands to do and words to cheer
>
> For Liberty and laws.[4]

## Revere's First Rides

On December 17, Paul Revere started out on horseback for New York and Philadelphia. Boston's town meeting, the city's governing body, had asked him to explain the "tea party" to groups in those cities. It was not his first ride for the patriots. The month before, he had ridden to seaports near Boston with news of the first tea ship's arrival. His round trip to New York and Philadelphia took ten days. On December 27, John Boyle, a Bostonian, wrote: "Mr. Paul Revere returned from New York and Philadelphia, performing his journey in a much shorter time then could be expected at this Season of the year."[5]

It took a mail carrier during this period six to nine days to carry a letter from Boston to New York. To take the letter on to Philadelphia would add at least a day more. Not only that, but the mail carriers were employees of the British government. For the patriot leaders in Massachusetts, it was faster and safer to use Paul Revere. Revere had a horse, he could ride fast, and he was able to explain what was going on in Massachusetts to patriots in other colonies.

Governor Hutchinson sent an account of the Boston Tea Party to Britain. Parliament responded in

### And the Roads Were Bad, Too

Philadelphia is about three hundred miles from Boston over modern highways, but no highways existed in Paul Revere's day. His route would have been longer, and the roads he traveled outside the towns would have been unpaved. New England roads were considered the best in the colonies, but they had many bad stretches.

"Very often we were surprised by a family of pigs taking a bath in a gully of sufficient compass to admit the coach," writes an Englishman of a stretch of road south of Boston.[6] And that was thirty years *after* Revere made his rides.

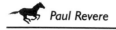 

1774 with what Bostonians called "The Intolerable Acts." One closed the port of Boston to everything but troops and military supplies. Another took control of the local government and the courts out of the hands of the colonists and gave it to men appointed by the British government. A third allowed Massachusetts offenders to be tried in Britain, not the colonies.

But that was not all. Governor Hutchinson was removed as governor of Massachusetts. He was replaced by General Thomas Gage, the commander of the British armed forces in the North American colonies. Gage took up residence in Boston and with him came British troops. By fall there would be some three thousand of them. An act was passed that allowed the troops to be housed, not just on Boston Common and in vacant buildings, but in people's homes. The city was under a military government.

The wharves, usually so noisy, were silent. The ships that were once tied up there were absent. On just about every street there were Redcoats. In North Square, several British marines were living with neighbors of the Reveres. The Reveres did not have any soldiers in their house; it was already crowded.

Revere's business suffered, as did the business of every other tradesman and merchant in Boston. Many people left the city. But the Revere family stayed.

Even though Revere had little business, he was busier than ever in 1774. He would make four round trips to New York and Philadelphia during the spring, summer, and fall. In May, he went to those two cities to carry Samuel Adams's request that the colonies stop all commerce with Britain. The other colonies were reluctant to do this, but some leaders proposed a congress, or meeting, of all the colonies to discuss their problems with Britain. A congress like this had never been held before in the colonies. The First Continental Congress opened in Philadelphia in September. In the opening address, Patrick Henry of Virginia told the delegates that "All America is one mass."[7]

Paul Revere would make three more trips to Philadelphia in 1774 in connection with the Congress. The weather on these trips was good, since the Congress was held in warm months. But when he took a trip to Portsmouth, New Hampshire, in the middle of December, the roads were covered with snow and ice. In addition, Paul and Rachel Revere's first child, Joshua, had been born the week before. Nevertheless, Revere felt he had to go. General Gage, the Massachusetts patriots had learned, planned to send soldiers to a fort in Portsmouth that held a large store of gunpowder.

Portsmouth is sixty miles from Boston. Revere made it in a day, reaching the city before the British

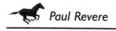
troops. The local militia rushed to the fort, which had only a few Regulars, and took them prisoner. Then they removed the gunpowder as well as a number of guns.

Revere made his way home to Rachel, the baby, and his six other children. In December 1774, he celebrated his fortieth birthday.

## General Gage Has a Plan

The rest of the winter was quiet in the colonies. But on April 7, the residents of Boston noticed some unusual activity around the ships in the harbor.[8] The small boats carried by the troop transports that had brought the Regulars to Boston had been launched. They were tied up under the sterns (backs) of the warships. Then the Bostonians were informed by patriots outside the city that British officers had been checking the roads to Concord, a town eighteen miles from Boston. The local militia had stored gunpowder and arms at Concord.

John Hancock and Samuel Adams were, at that very moment, staying in Lexington, which was a dozen miles from Boston on the road that led to Concord.

Revere discussed these facts with Joseph Warren. General Gage, they decided, was getting ready for something in the neighborhood of Concord and Lexington. For Revere, a ride of twelve or eighteen miles was a short jaunt compared to the long rides he had taken. He decided to visit the two towns to give his information to local patriots as well as to Hancock and Adams. So in the next week he took two rides, one to Concord and the other to Lexington. Both trips were uneventful.[9]

Revere had been forming a plan to alert patriots beyond Boston should he be unable to leave the city. On April 16, 1774, as he returned from his second trip, he met with a friend, Colonel William Conant, in Charlestown, across the Charles River from Boston. "I agreed . . . that if the British went out by water, we would shew [sic] two lanthorns [sic] in the North Church steeple," he wrote many years later, "and if by land, one, as a signal. . . ."[10] When the patriots in Charlestown saw this signal, they were to wait for Revere's arrival but be ready to spread the alarm themselves if he failed to arrive.

Revere had chosen the North Church near his home to display the lanterns because it was the highest building in Boston at that time. Its steeple could easily be seen from Charlestown.

Sometime during the next few days, Revere contacted three Boston friends, one of whom, Robert Newman, did maintenance work at North Church. He had the keys to the church. All agreed to the lantern plan. Then Revere and the rest of Boston waited to see what developed. On Tuesday, April 18, it became obvious that the British were

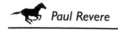 

finally planning a move. Troops were assembling on Boston Common as small boats lined up along the shore. On the afternoon of the eighteenth, Revere alerted his three friends to be ready that night to hang the lanterns.[11]

But what was the destination of the British troops? Joseph Warren had a spy who was very close to General Gage. But Warren could only call on the spy in emergencies. This was an emergency, he decided. He contacted the spy and learned the destination and mission of the troops. Warren immediately sent for Revere, who arrived sometime between nine and ten o'clock at night. Without revealing the spy's name, Warren told Revere the spy's message. The British planned to seize Hancock and Adams and burn the gunpowder and arms stored at Concord.

Warren had already sent this message to Lexington via another messenger, William Dawes. He had taken the land route over Boston Neck to Lexington. Warren chose the land route for Dawes because he often went through the military check point at the Neck in the course of his work. The sentries knew him. Revere would follow the route he had just taken to Lexington and Concord. It would take him by boat across the Charles to Charlestown, where he would pick up the road to Lexington. Warren gave Revere the same written message he had given Dawes.

"A large body of the King's troops (supposed to be a brigade of about 12, or 1500) were embarked in boats from Boston, and gone to land at Lechmere's point."[12]

It was about ten o'clock as Revere left Warren. He went to Robert Newman's house, which was across from North Church. Looking in the window of the Newman house, Revere saw several British officers playing cards at a table. The Newmans ran a boarding house and a number of Regulars were in residence. Just then someone stepped out of the shadows. It was Newman; with him were the other two men. Revere told them to hang two lanterns now. Then he left them.

Revere's home was only a few blocks away. He put on a long riding coat and a pair of heavy boots with spurs. It was about 10:15 P.M. when he left for the river. He did not ride a horse. We do not know if Revere owned a horse at this time, but even if he did, he could not have taken it across the Charles River in a small boat. He could only

*Joseph Warren sent Paul Revere on his famous ride on the night of April 18, 1775. Warren later became a general in the Massachusetts army.*

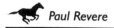 

hope that if he reached the other side, his friends would be able to find a good horse for him.

Revere's boat was concealed beneath a wharf on the Charles River. He had already arranged for two friends to row him across the water. They met him near the boat.

Within a few minutes, the three were in the small boat and rowing out into the Charles. The oars had been muffled by tying cloths around them. The moon, almost full, had begun to rise. In its light, a huge dark shape loomed up out of the water. It was the *Somerset*, the biggest warship in Boston Harbor, and she was anchored right in their path. Aboard it, Revere knew, lookouts would be on the alert for boats such as their own. No boats were allowed to cross the harbor after 9:00 P.M.

But that night, the moon remained so low on the horizon that it was partly hidden by the buildings of Boston. A dark moonshadow fell on Revere's boat and the three men inside it. The boat passed safely by the *Somerset*.

Charlestown and the road to Lexington lay ahead of Paul Revere.

# 6

# WORKING FOR THE REVOLUTION

Paul Revere was successful in warning the town of Lexington on the night of April 18, but he was stopped on his way to Concord. His warning, however, was carried to Concord and beyond by others. By dawn, militiamen were gathering on Lexington Green outside the Buckman Tavern. As Revere helped carry John Hancock's trunk away from the tavern, he heard the first shot of the American Revolution.

That first shot was quickly followed by others. On the Green, some sixty militiamen and several hundred Regulars were confronting each other.

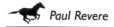 

When the brief fight was over, eight militiamen lay dead. One, who lived across the Green, dragged himself to his own doorstep and died. Another nine were wounded. The British had only one man wounded. With drums beating, the victors marched on to Concord, six miles away. It was six o'clock in the morning.

The several hundred Regulars who had faced the militiamen at Lexington were just the advance guard. In all, about seven hundred Regulars headed to Concord.

But thanks to the warnings of Revere, Dawes, and Prescott, many militiamen were headed there too. Prescott had galloped into Concord very early that morning. By the time the British reached the town, there was a growing crowd of militiamen on a hill above the Concord River. Below them was North Bridge. The Regulars put guards on the bridges and began to look for military supplies. They found very little. Paul Revere's earlier warning had resulted in most of the supplies being removed and hidden.

When the number of colonial militiamen had reached about five hundred, their commander gave the order to march on North Bridge. A young fifer walked in front, playing a lively British march. The Regulars withdrew to the far side of the bridge and went into one of the formations British troops used in combat. The men formed a block, with the front line down on one knee, ready to fire. The militiamen marched on. Several Regulars in the front line fired without a command. An American officer fell dead; the fifer was wounded.

The command of "Fire" rang out from militia officers. Four British officers were hit and a dozen soldiers killed or wounded. Their formation had made them easy targets. To the astonishment of the militiamen, the Regulars turned and ran.

## The Battle of Lexington

By late morning, the British commander in Concord realized that the number of militia was growing hourly. He ordered a retreat back to Boston, almost twenty miles away. The wounded were put into two carriages. As the Regulars marched back down the narrow road between Concord and Lexington, the militia followed them through the fields and woods. Soon there were an estimated one thousand militiamen pursuing the red-coated troops up the road.

At several spots, the militia commanders set up ambushes, firing at the Regulars from behind trees, walls, and houses. The Regulars were like a "whale attacked by sharks," as two historians put it.[1] Red-coated bodies were left lying on the road after each encounter. A large proportion of them were officers. The militiamen recognized the uniforms of officers and aimed at them. By the time Lexington was in sight, the surviving Regulars were frightened, exhausted, and almost out of ammunition.

Luckily for them, General Gage had decided to send reinforcements to Concord. When the Regulars reached Lexington Green, they met a brigade of British infantry with cannons. The reinforcements enabled the British troops to fight their way back to Boston. But British casualties far exceeded those of the militiamen. The colonials had won what came to be called the Battle of Lexington.

*This print of the action on Lexington Green was made by two artists who came to Lexington to participate in the fight.*

Paul Revere's whereabouts during the Battle of Lexington are not known. The trunk he was hiding as the battle started survived, however, and is now in Worcester Historical Museum in Worcester, Massachusetts.

Revere did not return to Boston after the battle. The patriot leaders were in danger from the moment the Regulars and the militiamen began to shoot at each other. Revere could not appear in Boston without running the risk of being arrested. Instead he went to Cambridge, where the Patriot's Committee of Safety, which was now the governing body for the colony of Massachusetts, was meeting. Rachel Revere and the children remained in Boston. No one could leave the city without a pass, which had to be obtained from General Gage's officers.

Revere and his wife sent each other a number of letters during this period. In one, Revere spells out the actions his "dear girl" should take to join him. "If you find you cannot easily get a pass for the Boat, I would have you get a pass for yourself and children and effects. Send the most valuable first. I mean . . . Beds enough for yourself and Children, my chest, your trunk, with Books Cloaths [sic] &c to the ferry tell the ferryman they are mine. I will provide a house where to put them . . ."[2]

At the end, he added: "I want some linen and stockings very much."[3]

*Paul Revere carried this pass when he was a messenger to the Second Continental Congress meeting in Philadelphia in the fall of 1775. The pass asks those who meet Revere to assist him with "horses or any other things he may stand in need of." James Otis signed the pass.*

A short time later, Rachel Revere replied that as far as the pass was concerned, "I am almost sure of one as soon as they are given out. . . ."[4] Rachel was a busy woman, the letter shows. The letter refers to payments she is trying to collect from customers, coats she is trying to have made for Revere and son Paul, and to "2 bottles beer 1 wine" with which she is bribing a Captain Irvin to obtain the pass.[5] In her letter, as in her husband's, the affection between the husband and wife is plain. "do take care of yourself," she bursts out in the middle of the letter.[6]

During this period when it was so difficult to leave or enter Boston, one man seemed to have no trouble doing it. He was Dr. Benjamin Church, who was a member of many of the same groups as Revere. He carried some of the Revere letters back and forth from Boston to Cambridge. On one occasion, Rachel Revere gave him a letter to her husband and one hundred twenty-five pounds, a large sum in those days. Paul Revere never received them.

### What Happened to Rachel Revere's Letter

Dr. Benjamin Church, an old friend of Paul Revere's, was made Surgeon General for General Washington's new Army. Church's office was right across the street from General Washington's headquarters in the summer of 1775. In September, a coded letter Church had sent to one of General Gage's officers in Boston was turned over to Washington. At a court-martial, a military trial, Church was found guilty of secret correspondence with the British.

The sentence was a light one: exile in the islands of the British West Indies. The ship carrying Church to the West Indies disappeared in a storm.

Many years later, the letter Rachel Revere had given to Dr. Church for her husband in 1775 was found among General Gage's papers. The hundred twenty-five pounds was not with it.

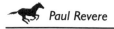 

## Revere Rides Again

Sometime in May 1775, however, Rachel and all the children left Boston. Paul Revere found quarters for them in Watertown, seven miles from Boston. A few days after the Battle of Lexington, he began to work as a messenger again. He carried a letter with news of the battle and a request for help in raising an army to towns in Massachusetts. The Committee of Safety paid him four shillings a day (he had asked for five). Revere's messenger work, and that of others, succeeded. Men turned out by the thousands to enlist in new regiments that were being formed.

The recruitment of all these men soon gave Revere another job: printing money to pay them. Up until this time, the colonists had used British money: pounds, shillings, pennies, and other bills and coins of the British realm. Now that they were fighting Britain, they needed their own money. Paper bills were the easiest money to make and who better to make them than Paul Revere? He had his own copper plates, printing press, and tools, and he was an experienced engraver.

Unfortunately, all his equipment was in Boston. But somehow, Revere got it out. He may have arranged to hide it in one of the wagons that brought food to the city. By May 1775, he was hard at work in Watertown, turning out bills for different amounts. He used the backs of some of his old

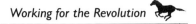

**THIRTYSIX-SHILLINGS.**

Decm.ʳ 7. 1775.

*This is one of the notes Paul Revere printed up for the new Massachusetts government in 1775. The Americans still used the British monetary system.*

copper plates to engrave the bills. The work of printing money was so important—and so dangerous—that a military guard protected him around the clock.

The Second Continental Congress was meeting in Philadelphia at this time. It authorized the raising of an army to help Massachusetts and named George Washington of Virginia as its head. On the very day—June 15—that the Congress took these steps, General Gage was making plans to seize Bunker Hill, across the Charles River in Charlestown. When the patriots heard about his plans, they decided to take Bunker Hill themselves. On the evening of June 16, 1775, patriot troops moved in. They decided to make their stand on an adjoining hill, Breed's Hill.

## The Battle of Breed's Hill

When General Gage learned what had happened, he began ferrying British troops to Charlestown. While

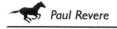 

this was going on, the colonials on Breed's Hill welcomed a volunteer: Dr. Joseph Warren. Although he had just been named a general in the Massachusetts army, he fought as an ordinary soldier that day. The battle began around noon. As the patriots hid behind barriers they had built, Redcoats charged up the hill. General Israel Putnam of Connecticut is said to have shouted "Don't fire till you see the whites of their eyes!" during the battle.[7]

The patriots managed to throw back two waves of Redcoats, but a third wave made it over the hill. The colonial troops fled, leaving their dead—some one hundred and forty men—behind. One of the dead was Dr. Warren. But the British had much higher losses than the colonials that day. A total of 226 British soldiers were killed and 828 wounded out of 2,000 troops.

That fall, Paul Revere was given another important responsibility. In November, he traveled to Pennsylvania to look at the only gunpowder mill in the colonies. Gunpowder was desperately needed by the colonies. The patriot leaders in Massachusetts hoped Revere could learn enough to start a powder mill in Massachusetts. The owner of the mill gave Revere only a quick tour but Revere picked up most of the information he needed. The rest was supplied by a diagram of the mill Samuel Adams was able to obtain. Soon another mill was in operation.

Meanwhile, General Washington had been analyzing the situation around Boston. He realized he would have the British under his thumb if only he could get some cannons to a high place overlooking the city. The most likely place was Dorchester Heights. General Washington had no cannons to spare, but there were cannons at Fort Ticonderoga on Lake Champlain in New York, which had been captured by patriot troops. That winter, sleds hauled the cannons all the way to the Boston area. Soon they were in place on Dorchester Heights and so were some four thousand men.

On March 2, 1776, a bombardment of Boston began. Now General William Howe, who had replaced General Gage, was in an even worse predicament than General Gage had been with Breed's Hill.

Howe was a decisive man. On March 17, St. Patrick's Day, the British left Boston, along with some one thousand civilians who remained loyal to Britain.

After almost a year, Paul Revere and the other citizens of Boston could go home.

# DISGRACE FOR PAUL REVERE

Paul Revere and his family had been away from Boston for almost a year. When they returned in March of 1776, they were shocked at the condition of the city. Almost no trees were left along the streets; all had been cut down for firewood by the British troops. The Liberty Tree was just a stump. The search for firewood had also resulted in a number of buildings being torn down. Others had their paneling and floors ripped out. The buildings that were left intact needed paint and repairs.

The Revere house in North Square, however, had come through the period without much damage. Revere's shop was in good condition, too, perhaps because it had been rented to an Englishman.

One of the first things Paul Revere did after he returned was take a boat across the Charles River to Charlestown. Joseph Warren's two brothers went with him. Someone had told them the general location of Warren's grave and the fact that he had been buried with a farmer wearing a certain kind of shirt. The three men found a grave with two bodies, one wearing a shirt of the kind described to them. The skull of the other body had several false teeth. Revere himself had placed false teeth in Joseph Warren's mouth. When Revere examined the teeth, he saw they were held in place by a silver wire. He recognized the wire; it came from his shop.

They took Warren's body back to Boston, where a funeral attended by most of Boston was held at King's Chapel. He was buried in the Old Granary, the cemetery where Revere's father and first wife were buried.

George Washington left Boston only a few days after the British did. He took most of the Massachusetts troops with him. Later Paul Revere told one of his friends that he had hoped for a commission in the Continental Army. But it was never offered to him.[1] Instead, Massachusetts gave him a commission as a lieutenant colonel of artillery

in its forces. He was put in charge of Fort William on Castle Island. This was the island in Boston Harbor where British sympathizers had lived during the period when the Sons of Liberty were active.

## Massachusetts Becomes a State

That summer, John Hancock sent a friend in Boston a copy of a document that had been signed by the members of the Continental Congress on July 4, 1776. John Hancock's signature was the biggest of all. The document had been written by a young Virginian, Thomas Jefferson, and it was called The Declaration of Independence. One line read: "These United Colonies are, and of Right ought to be Free and Independent States."[2] From then on, the colony of Massachusetts would be known as the state of Massachusetts.

On April 30, 1777, Rachel Revere had her third son. They named him Joseph Warren. Rachel's second son had died, so she now had added two sons to the household. A few weeks later, on May 23, Paul Revere's mother, Deborah Hitchborn Revere, died after a long illness. She was seventy-four.

News of the Revolutionary War slowly trickled into Boston. The British occupied Philadelphia, but its loss was balanced by a big victory at Saratoga, New York, in the fall of 1777. A quarter of the British army—almost six thousand men—surrendered. This was a victory the Bostonians could identify with because as a result, the British withdrew all their troops in the northern states into Canada. Now, in the North, they occupied only Rhode Island, New York City, and Philadelphia. They would not try to take Boston again.

Of course the Bostonians did not know that in the fall of 1777. Nevertheless, the victory at Saratoga made everyone in Boston breathe easier.

Out on Castle Island, however, the energetic Paul Revere had little to do. He presided at numerous court-martials, he kept the cannons in good repair, and he wrote letters asking for modest increases in supplies. In 1778, he addressed a letter to the State of Massachusetts complaining about the cost of uniforms for himself and the other officers. He asked for "As much Blue Cloth as will make each a Coat with trimmings . . . some White Woolen or Linnen [sic] cloth for Waistcoat & Breeches, Two pair of stockings, Linnen for two Shirts . . ."[3]

## The French Join the New United States

Soon came news that promised activity for the bored men on Castle Island. In the spring of 1778, France joined the new nation of the United States in the battle against Britain. Individual Frenchmen like the Marquis de Lafayette, who was on General Washington's staff, had given their services to the colonies. But now France was officially on the side of the United States.

The first French ship, the *Nymphile*, sailed into Boston Harbor in March of 1778. On Castle Island, Paul Revere was ordered to "fire the Heavy Cannon on Castle Island when the French Frigate passes by the Castle Provided she Salutes the same."[4]

Soon a whole French fleet entered Boston Harbor. The French officers were entertained by John Hancock in his grand mansion. He had resigned his post as president of the Continental Congress and returned to Boston. In the summer of 1778, the Americans and the French made plans for a joint expedition against the British in Rhode Island. Troops from the Continental Army would take part, along with men from the militias of Massachusetts, Rhode Island, and Connecticut. Paul Revere would have a role as the commander of the artillery from Fort William.

By August, the troops were in Rhode Island. But there they were hit by one of the worst storms ever recorded in that region. The French and English fleets were scattered by the winds, making it impossible for the French fleet to help the Americans. The French ships sailed back to Boston. The American troops marched home. That fall, the French fleet left Boston. The British fleet, which had been hovering nearby, was hit by another storm. The *Somerset*, the same ship

Revere was rowed by before his famous ride, was wrecked on Cape Cod, Massachusetts.

In March 1779, Revere was in charge of removing the *Somerset's* sixty-four big guns. Revere managed to salvage twenty-one. They were hauled to Boston for use in the city's defense.

That summer, the state of Massachusetts received alarming news. A British force of some seven hundred men had landed at Penobscot Bay in Maine. Maine was then part of Massachusetts. The British had begun to build a fort there. All of Massachusetts was in an uproar at the news. Penobscot Bay was only one hundred fifty miles north of Boston. With forts at Penobscot Bay and Newport, Rhode Island, the

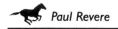 

British could control shipping on the whole northeastern coast of the United States.

## The Penobscot Expedition

Something had to be done, Massachusetts leaders told the Continental Congress. The Congress agreed. A major land and sea expedition against Penobscot Bay was quickly planned. The Congress contributed the largest ship, the thirty-two-gun *Warren*, plus two other ships. New Hampshire contributed a ship. Massachusetts enlisted its whole navy, three ships. In addition, a dozen privateers, armed private vessels, joined up. The armed vessels carried some two thousand sailors, and unarmed transport ships carried about one thousand soldiers.

The leader of the expedition was Dudley Saltonstall of the Continental Navy. Solomon Lovell led the land forces. Paul Revere was put in charge of the artillery for the land forces—seven cannons.

The expedition moved out of Boston on July 21, 1779. Three days later the ships sailed into Penobscot Bay. Revere wrote in his diary: "I could plainly see with my Glass [telescope], the enemy had begun a Fort, on one of the Heights. . . ."[6] Three small ships protected the fort, which was only about half-finished. Fort George, as the British had named it (for King George III), seemed like an easy target for the expedition from Boston.

A few days after their arrival, General Lovell led a force up the steep slope on which Fort George was built. It was so steep that Paul Revere and his men were unable to haul their heavy guns with them. Revere found the only way he could get himself up was by hanging onto branches and pulling himself up. Eventually, however, the Americans reached the heights. They defeated a small party of defenders who came out of the fort.

General Lovell and his men had established themselves about six hundred yards in front of the fort when the attack stalled. Lovell, who had lost a number of men, wanted Captain Saltonstall to bombard the fort before Lovell's men moved in. The captain wanted General Lovell to attack the fort before the ships moved closer. While the wrangling went on, Revere and his men made a road and hauled some of their guns up to the American line.

The British were busy too. They worked feverishly on their unfinished fort.

Early in August, a speedy boat arrived from Boston. It brought bad news. The Navy Board in Philadelphia had learned that a British naval force was on the way from New York to Penobscot Bay. The boat also carried an order from the Navy Board for Captain Saltonstall. It ended: "It is our order that as soon as you receive this you make the most effectual measures for the capture or destruction of

the enemy's ships."[7] Saltonstall could not ignore a direct order from the Navy Board, his employer. He made plans to attack on August 13, 1779.

At dawn on that day, everything was ready. General Lovell had moved closer to the fort. Captain Saltonstall had placed his ships in position. Gunners stood by their guns, ready to fire. A morning fog lifted. But just as Captain Saltonstall, aboard the *Warren*, was ready to give the order to fire on the British ships and the fort, a ship drew alongside the *Warren*. It was the *Diligent*, one of the three ships from the Continental Navy, and the crew members had an alarming message. They had spotted several large ships coming up the bay. It was the British fleet.

## Disaster on the Penobscot

Captain Saltonstall ordered cannons and troops back onto the transport ships and sent them up the Penobscot River. When the British fleet came into view, Saltonstall made one of his rare quick decisions. He ordered the warships underway. They sailed past the slow transports, leaving the unarmed ships to fend for themselves. The captains of the transports panicked. They grounded their ships on the shores of the Penobscot River. The troops leaped out. It was, as Revere wrote, "utmost confusion."[8]

During that day and the following night, all the ships in the American fleet were either captured by the British or burned by their captains to avoid capture. Revere and some of his men camped out in the woods for the night, then walked to the Kennebeck River. From there they made their way to an American outpost. Revere's last entry in his diary reads: "I got to Fort Western where I found most of my Officers and men; after supplying them with what money I could spare, I ordered them to Boston by the nearest route."[9] Then he took off on foot for Boston himself.

When Revere and the men from the Penobscot Expedition arrived back in Boston, they were not victors. They were the survivors of the worst naval

### The Wrecks in the Penobscot

In the twentieth century, the remains of the *Warren*, the biggest ship in the Penobscot Expedition, were found at the bottom of the Penobscot River. A bronze cannon was removed from the wreck. It had the Massachusetts state seal that is said to have been designed by Paul Revere. He had visited a cannon-making plant in 1777, and he may have made some cannons used on the Penobscot Expedition. The remains of several other ships on the expedition have also been found in the river. The *Defence*, a privateer, is the only one that has been excavated. Items from the ship are at the Maine State Museum in Augusta.

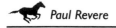 

defeat in American history. Because of the lack of coordination of the land and sea attack, they had lost not only some five hundred men but all their ships, cannons, guns, and supplies as well. The state of Massachusetts figured the bill for the expedition to be 7 million dollars. In Massachusetts, just about everyone was angry with the men of the expedition for the way they had handled what had seemed like a sure victory. General Washington was critical too.

Paul Revere had taken up his duties out on Castle Island as soon as he returned. Two weeks later, on September 6, 1779, the State of Massachusetts passed an order that Lieutenant Colonel Paul Revere resign the command of Castle Island and "repair to his dwelling house in Boston and there continue till the matter complained of can be duly enquired into."[10] A marine captain, Thomas Carnes, had filed a complaint against Revere for "disobedience of orders" and "unsoldierlike behaviour [sic] tending to cowardice" on the expedition.[11] Peleg Wadsworth, an American general, had also criticized Revere's behavior.

Wadsworth's charges carried more weight, since he was the second in command of the land forces. Wadsworth maintained that Revere had failed to obey his orders on the retreat up the Penobscot.[12]

Paul Revere's only military campaign during the Revolutionary War had ended in disgrace.

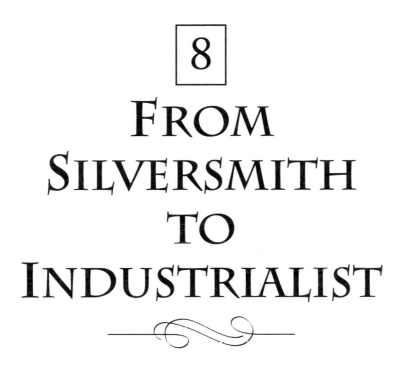

# 8

# FROM SILVERSMITH TO INDUSTRIALIST

Paul Revere was not the only member of the Penobscot Expedition to be criticized after he returned home. There were many complaints about Captain Saltonstall's leadership and about General Lovell's, too. The General Court of Massachusetts set up a committee to investigate the charges against the three men. The committee put most of the blame for what happened on Saltonstall. He was found guilty at a court-martial and dismissed from the Continental Navy.

Although the charges against Lovell and Revere were dismissed, Revere was reprimanded for his

behavior. He was not given back his post at Castle Island.

Paul Revere blamed the charges against him on measures he had taken against soldiers who had deserted from Castle Island to join privateers. The privateer captains, Revere maintained, were trying to get revenge for Revere's efforts to get his soldiers back. The arguments Revere had with several members of the Penobscot Expedition probably played a role in the charges against him too. Revere had strong views and he expressed them strongly.

Revere wrote to the committee several times, demanding a court-martial to clear his name. But the committee put him off.

Revere's dismissal from Castle Island was a low point in his life. But it did give him more time for his business. His account books show that in 1779, the year he left Castle Island, he began to sell items from his shop again. Young Paul, who had been serving on Castle Island, too, was back working as an apprentice for his father again. But business was poor. Boston's trade had been ruined by the war, and few people could afford silver teapots or even buckles. In 1780, the Reveres rented their North Square house, probably because they needed cash.

Revere referred to his finances in a letter he sent to the General Court of Massachusetts in 1780. He asked for back rations that, he said, he had not received since June of 1779. "I have been maintaining a Family of twelve ever since, out of the remains of what I have earned by twenty years hard labor."[1]

During this period, Revere began to write to his Rivoire cousins in France and on the English island of Guernsey. Apollos Rivoire, Paul Revere's father, had lived with the Guernsey Rivoires briefly before leaving for America. Revere's cousin in France, Matthias, wrote in French, and Paul Revere wrote in English; they had each other's letters translated. John Rivoire, Revere's cousin on Guernsey, not only wrote and spoke English but had English views. His first letter attacked the French and suggested America rejoin the "Mother Country"—Britain.

Paul Revere replied in his usual strong way to his cousin. He himself had been prejudiced against the French but now found them "brave, humane, generous, and polite."[2] In response to his cousin's suggestion that America rejoin Britain, Revere wrote: "I do assure you the name of an Englishman is as odious to an American, as that of a Turk or a Savage. You may depend that the Americans will never submit to be under the Brittons again."[3] After this spirited defense, Revere invited his cousin to visit him in America. John Rivoire never did accept his cousin's invitation, but the two cousins exchanged several more letters. The letters show that neither changed his opinion.

While Paul Revere was struggling to make a living in Boston, the war dragged on further south. France was an ally of the United States, but she had been unable to help in a significant way. In 1781, the situation changed. That summer, the French informed General Washington that their fleet and thousands of troops were ready to come to his aid. Washington decided to fight a land and sea battle in Virginia, his home state. British general Charles Cornwallis had moved eight thousand troops to Yorktown, Virginia, a town on the James River. (The James flows into Chesapeake Bay.) Washington realized Cornwallis could be trapped if the French fleet kept the British fleet out of Chesapeake Bay.

While Washington led his men toward Yorktown, the French fleet set sail for the same destination. The battle began on September 30. Everything went as Washington had predicted. On October 19, 1781, Cornwallis surrendered his eight thousand men. Although this was the biggest victory the Americans had won, no one realized at first that it was the last major battle of the war. The British army still was in a strong position in New York.

Early in 1782, Paul Revere finally received his court-martial. Twelve captains and a general were appointed to the panel to hear the evidence. In the years since the Penobscot Expedition, both Revere's accusers and the accusations against him had dwindled. There were just two charges left. One had to do with his refusing to give up a boat to General Wadsworth on the retreat up the Penobscot. The other involved Revere's leaving the Penobscot without orders. The twelve captains and the general acquitted Revere on both, which meant he was not guilty. The findings were signed by John Hancock, who was now governor of Massachusetts.

While Paul Revere's court-martial was taking place, a crucial election was going on in Britain. The government that had prosecuted the war had fallen. The new government wanted peace. Negotiations between the United States and Britain began later that year. The formal end of the war was announced on April 19, 1783, eight years to the day after Revere had ridden into Lexington. The peace treaty was signed in September in Paris, France. The war that had started on Lexington Green was finally over.

Paul Revere was a patriot, and he rejoiced with other patriots at the end of the long war. But he was also a businessman whose family of twelve needed money. Even before the treaty was signed, he had an agent in Britain—a British sympathizer who had once lived in Boston—ship him a number of barrels of metal hardware. Some of these barrels contained tools he needed in his work, but others held consumer goods. He planned to sell these items, as well as ones he made himself, in a shop.

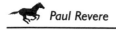 

In December of 1785, he put an advertisement in the *Massachusetts Sentinel* for the new shop:

> Imported and to be Sold, by Paul Revere, Directly opposite Liberty Pole, A General assortment of Hardware, consisting of Pewter, Brass, Copper, Ironmongery, Cutlery, Japaned and Plated Wares, Among which are a few neat Brass Sconces . . . 3-pint plated Coffee-Urns, and Goblets, Very neat japanned Tea Trays, in sets, Brass Candlesticks, Looking-Glasses . . . Carving Knives, &c. &c. All which will be sold at he lowest advance for cash . . .[4]

From the 1780s on, Revere probably spent most of his time at the hardware shop and, later, his other businesses. He left most of the silversmithing to his son Paul and others, although Revere controlled the style of the items they produced. Revere's books show that his silversmith shop turned out four times as many silver items in the postwar years as it did before the war. The biggest group of items was connected with tea drinking. Now that tea was readily available again, Bostonians drank more of it than ever. In 1792, the shop made a whole set of teaware, one of its biggest orders. It had eight pieces, plus eighteen spoons.

In 1786, Revere moved his silversmith shop and his retail shop to a new location in the center of Boston. From his front door, he could see the State House and the site in front of it where the Boston Massacre took place in 1770. By this time, his shop sold mainly hardware imported from England. In the same year Revere moved his shop, the first bridge from Boston to Charlestown was completed. Now Charlestown, where Revere had started his famous ride, could be reached in just a few minutes.

Soon Revere was no longer satisfied to be selling hardware made by others. In 1788, he set up a

### New Teapots for a New Nation

The teapots the Revere shop made during these postwar years look very different than the ones made before the war. After the war, the neoclassical style became popular. This style was meant to resemble the buildings and decorations of ancient Greece. So the Revere shop made teapots with straight sides instead of curved ones and engraved them with classical motifs such as garlands of flowers. Another kind of neoclassical teapot the Revere shop made after the war had ridges, or "flutes," on the sides.

The straight-sided and fluted teapots the Revere shop turned out after the war were made with sheet silver produced by machines. The silver sheets could be formed into a straight-sided shape such as a teapot without the lengthy process of flattening a silver bar with a hammer. Paul Revere, who was always interested in new technology, began making teapot spouts with sheet silver in the early 1780s. Teapots and other items soon followed. By 1785, Revere had a small mill built in his shop to turn out his own sheet silver.

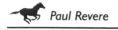 

*From the front door of his new hardware shop in the center of Boston, Paul Revere could see the State House. It was in front of this building that the Boston Massacre took place.*

small foundry on the North End waterfront. It probably made some of the hardware he sold, as well as larger items such as stoves. "We have got our furnass [sic] agoing, and find that it answers our expectations,"[5] he wrote to the firm that supplied him with the metal. The foundry, which was right next to shipyards, was soon supplying the yards with bolts, spikes, and nails used in building ships. Revere now spent most of his time at the foundry. He rented a house near the foundry and moved the silversmith shop to the North End, too.

By this time, Paul Revere was a grandfather. His daughter Deborah and his son Paul had both married. Each produced a big family. But there were still young children in the home of Paul and Rachel Revere. Joseph Warren Revere, who had been named for Revere's good friend, was twelve in 1788. His sisters Mary and Harriet and his brother John were all younger than he was. These younger sons went to the Latin school, not the writing school Paul Revere had attended. John went to Harvard College.

The year 1788, when Revere started his foundry, was the year the United States was struggling to pass a Constitution. Nine of the thirteen states had to pass the document to make it effective. By January 1788, five states had said yes to the document. In Massachusetts, it was still being discussed by the Constitutional Convention meeting in Boston. The convention was almost equally divided; no one could predict the vote. Revere, like most of the tradesmen in Boston,

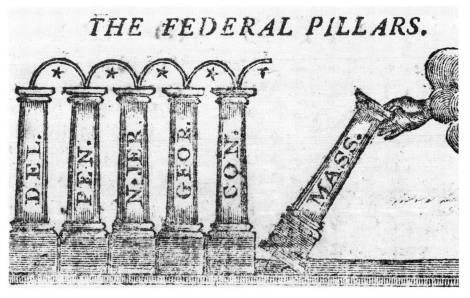

THE FEDERAL PILLARS.

*The* Centinel *newspaper ran this engraving to show how Massachusetts became the sixth state to ratify the Constitution. A pillar with the letters "MASS." is pushed into place next to pillars representing the other ratifying states. Below the pillars it says: "United They Stand—Divided Fall."*

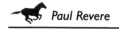 

wanted the Constitution to pass. These tradesmen believed the Constitution would make the nation more stable.

In January, the tradesmen held a meeting at the Green Dragon Tavern and voted unanimously for adoption. Paul Revere led a procession that took the results of the vote to Samuel Adams, a member of the convention. At Adams's house, Adams demanded more information.

"How many mechanics were at the Green Dragon when these resolutions were passed?"

"More, Sir," answered Revere, "than the Green Dragon could hold."

"And where were the rest, Mr. Revere?"

"In the streets, Sir."

"And how many were in the streets?"

"More, Sir, than there are stars in the sky."[6]

Samuel Adams and a majority of the Massachusetts convention voted to ratify the Constitution. It became the law of the land in the summer of 1788.

# CASTING
# BELLS AND
# COPPERING
# SHIPS

Paul Revere was not content for long making hardware and nails. In 1792, he took on a new challenge: making church bells.

It all started with the bell of his own church, the Cockerel. In 1792, the bell developed a crack, so that it could not be rung. Church bells were very important to Bostonians, calling them to services and ringing for other occasions as well. So when the Cockerel's bell was unable to be rung, some of the prominent members of the church held a meeting. Paul Revere attended the meetings. Throughout his life, Revere was always quick to offer his services to

resolve problems, and so it was again. After the various alternatives for dealing with the bell had been discussed, he offered to recast it himself. The offer was quickly accepted.

The only trouble was that Revere had no idea how to cast a bell. Only a few bells had ever been made in the United States, one of them the famous Liberty Bell of Philadelphia. Bell-making was a very specialized trade. The bell-maker had to mix copper, the principal metal in bells, with other metals in certain proportions to produce a good sound. Church bells were enormous, often weighing over a thousand pounds. They required giant molds into which the molten metal was poured. Revere had never cast anything bigger than a stove.

But he always liked a challenge. He remembered that in Abington, Massachusetts, a man named Aaron Hobart had set up a bell foundry before the Revolution. It had only produced a few bells before the war started. Revere brought Hobart's son and an employee of the Hobart Foundry to Boston. Using the copper from the old Cockerel bell, plus additional metal, the team cast a bell that weighed almost a thousand pounds. Revere was very proud of his first bell. On it, he engraved the words: "The first bell cast in Boston 1792 P. Revere."[1]

From then on, the Revere Foundry undertook any bell-making commissions it could obtain.

*Revere and his son, Joseph Warren, cast at least three hundred bells at their foundry. This one was cast in 1801, when Paul Revere was still very active in the business.*

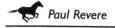 

Revere's new house near the foundry had a big yard where the bells were tested. A boy who lived near the Reveres remembered being in the yard with his friends while one of the big bells was being tested. Revere pushed the boys aside with his cane. "Take care, boys!" he cried. "if that hammer should hit your head, you'd ring louder than those bells do."[2]

At least three hundred bells were made by Paul Revere and his son Joseph Warren, who would carry on the foundry business after his father retired. Over a hundred are still in existence.

## Copper for a New Navy

Soon a new business opportunity opened up for Revere practically on his doorstep. His foundry was very close to the Hartt Shipyard, which received an order to build a forty-four-gun frigate for the brand-new United States Navy. A frigate was a fast, medium-sized sailing ship used for patrols and the destruction of enemy commerce. This frigate would be called the *Constitution*. There were plans to build a smaller Navy ship in Boston, too. United States merchant ships had been having trouble with pirates off the coast of North Africa, and new armed ships were being built to deal with the problem. Paul Revere had already been supplying bolts, spikes, and nails to Boston shipyards. Who better to supply the Navy with the other items it would need?

So Revere sat down and wrote the United States government a letter: "I understand that there are to be two Ships built in this State, for the General government, and that they are to be Coppered, if so, they will want *Composition bolts, Rudder braces* &c. . . . I will do them as cheap as any one, and as well."[3]

Revere got the order to supply copper and brass bolts, spikes, nails, and other items for the two ships. (He also made the Hartt family a tea service.) His bill for the *Constitution* came to $3,820.33, including the cost of a ship's bell.

In 1799, George Washington, who had served two terms as the first president of the United States, died. Bostonians always had a special affection for Washington. He had backed them when Massachusetts stood alone against the powerful nation of Great Britain. During the war, he had forced the British out of Boston. Revere felt especially close to Washington because both were Masons. In January 1800, Revere and several other Masons wrote Martha Washington, asking for a lock of her husband's hair.

Mrs. Washington sent the lock, and Paul Revere himself made a miniature gold urn to hold it. The urn, with its lock of hair, now belongs to the Grand Lodge of Masons in Massachusetts.

In 1800, when Paul Revere was sixty-five years old, he sold his house in North Square. The year before, he had bought a house near his foundry. The new house

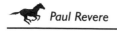 

was one a prosperous Boston family would occupy. Built of brick, it had three stories and stood on a large lot. The rooms were big and square and there were wide halls. In his house, Revere had some handsome pieces of furniture. One was a sideboard on which Rachel Revere could display a Revere tea service.

An artist made a profile drawing of Revere in 1800, when he visited Philadelphia. It shows a man with a full head of hair, although no longer dark, and a double chin. Revere had put on weight as he got older. A man who knew him then described him as "a thick-set, round faced, not very tall person, who always wore small-clothes."[4] By small clothes, he meant a shirt, vest, knee-length breeches, and long stockings but not a coat. Usually, a man would have worn these clothes inside his house or shop and put a coat over them when he went outside.

This clothing, however, was eighteenth century fashion. By 1800, fashionable men in Boston wore long, tight pants, high hats, and short coats. But Revere stuck to the clothes he had worn most of his life.

## A New Career

In more important ways, however, Paul Revere kept up with the times. In 1800, the year after he bought his new house, he bought a large piece of land in Canton, Massachusetts, about seventeen miles south of Boston. There he planned to establish a foundry to

### At Home in Canton

After Paul Revere established his foundry in Canton, the Revere family began spending part of their time there. Their Canton home was a simple two-story wooden house. Paul Revere had never lived in the country, but he liked Canton so well that he wrote a poem about it. It began:

> Not distant far from Taunton road
> In Canton dale is my abode.
> My Cot 'tho small, my mind's at ease,
> My Better Half, takes pains to please,
> Content sits lolling in her chair,
> And all my friends find welcome there . . .[5]

produce sheet copper, something no one in the United States had managed to do up to that date. Paul Revere was already a successful businessman, with his foundry and his silversmith shop. But at an age when many people retire today, he sank every penny he had into a risky new business venture.

Sheet copper refers to copper that comes in sheets of various thicknesses. Ever since the middle of the eighteenth century, sheet copper had been invaluable to the British navy. The copper was attached to the bottom of wooden sailing ships to prevent worms from eating holes in the wood and barnacles from clinging to the ship. Although not as destructive as the worms, the barnacles slowed the

ships down. The French navy soon began using copper on its ships, too.

Naturally, the United States Navy wanted to use sheet copper. But no one in the United States made it. It was imported from Britain. When Britain and France went to war again in 1793, however, sheet copper became hard to get. That was when Revere got the idea of making it himself. He already had a market in the United States Navy, if he could only learn the secret of rolling out copper to the thickness necessary for sheets. Revere had spent many years rolling out silver sheets, but copper sheets for a large ship were a very different proposition.

Nevertheless, Revere apparently did use a silver rolling mill to roll out some experimental sheets. The sheets he produced impressed the United States government enough for them to give Revere a ten-thousand-dollar loan to set up a copper rolling mill at Canton. With about fifteen thousand dollars of his own money and the government loan, Revere set up a mill. In 1801, Revere wrote the secretary of the Navy, saying: "I have erected my Works & have Rolled Sheet Copper which is approved of by the best judges as being equal to the best Cold Rolled Copper."[6] His big gamble had paid off.

Revere's first major customer was not the United States Navy, however, but the state of Massachusetts.

*Paul Revere furnished copper for the* Constitution, *including covering the whole bottom of the ship with sheets of copper. The first ship built for the United States Navy, the* Constitution *is now a museum in Boston Harbor.*

In 1802, Revere sheet copper was used to cover the dome on the roof of the new State House. It had been erected on what had been land belonging to John Hancock.

The following year, the *Constitution* was hauled into dry dock in Boston and its bottom coppered with Revere copper. This ship would be the flagship of Commodore Edward Preble during the war with the pirates of North Africa. Later it would play an important role in the War of 1812.

Another famous early customer of the Revere copper works was Robert Fulton of New York. He bought very thick copper sheets to make the boilers for his new steamships.

## Paul Revere and Son

In 1804, Revere wrote a friend that the new mill was "a tolerable advantageous business." He added: "I have my son in partnership with me."[7] Joseph

Warren ran the Boston foundry and his father the Canton foundry. In 1804, the Boston foundry was closed after it was damaged by a hurricane. The equipment was moved to Canton.

During these Canton years, Paul Revere seems to have gradually discontinued his work with the silversmith shop. The last piece of silver known to have been made by him is a pitcher dated 1806.

In 1811, Paul Revere was seventy-seven years old. He had already lived longer than most people did in those days. It was time, he decided, to turn

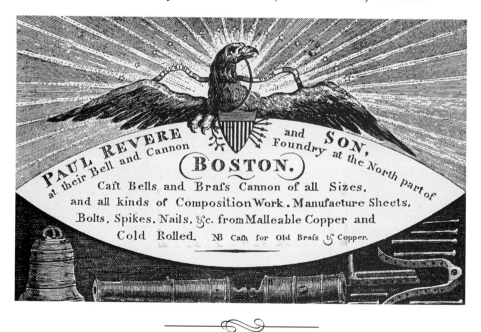

*This is a business card for Paul Revere and his son, Joseph Warren. This card was made in the late eighteenth or early nineteenth century when the Reveres' Boston foundry was in operation.*

**Paul Revere's Children**

Paul Revere had sixteen children, but only five were living when their father died. They were Mary, Joseph Warren, Harriet, Maria, and John. Mary was a child of Paul Revere's first marriage to Sarah Orne; the others were children of his second marriage. Joseph Warren, who was already running his father's business, continued that role. He also served in the Massachusetts legislature. The longest-lived child of Paul Revere, he died in 1868 at the age of ninety-two. One of his sons became president of the family firm. Joseph Warren's two other sons fought and died in the Civil War.

John, Revere's youngest child, who was a doctor when his father died, later became a professor of medicine at the University of the City of New York. His son, Joseph Warren, served as a brigadier general in the Civil War.

the business over to Joseph Warren. By this time, Paul Revere was a rich man. He was not as wealthy as John Hancock, who had died in 1793, or as the new Boston merchants such as the Lowells and the Cabots. But he was a prosperous man with a large house, good furniture, and money to spare. Rachel Revere could now sit "lolling in her chair" as the poem Revere wrote describes her doing.[8]

Rachel Revere died in 1813. Her stepson, Paul, who had worked with his father for so long in the silversmith shop, died the same year.

Paul Revere's health remained good. In 1814, during the War of 1812, Bostonians were called on to help build a fort to defend the city from British landing parties. Revere, who was eighty, signed up to help. He also offered the services of his workers in Canton. The British never did land in Boston, but there was a battle between a British ship and an American ship in Boston Harbor. In 1815, there was peace again.

The following year, Paul Revere made his will. Five of his children were still living, and each of them received the same sum. The rest of the money was divided among the grandchildren. Almost all of Revere's children had big families; some forty children had been born by 1816. The will also gave Joseph Warren the chance to buy out his brothers' and sisters' shares in the copper mill at Canton.

In 1817, the Revere foundry recast the bell for King's Chapel, the church where Dr. Joseph Warren's funeral was held so long before. At 2,437 pounds, this bell was the biggest ever cast by Revere. It is also said to have the finest sound. The King's Chapel bell was Boston's "passing bell," rung whenever someone died. From the number of times the bell rang, listeners could tell whether the deceased was a man or woman and how old he or she was. The bell was rehung in the bell tower in early 1818.

On May 10, 1818, Paul Revere died at the age of eighty-three. The bell in King's Chapel tolled for him.

# 10

# A NEW ROLE FOR REVERE: HERO

Paul Revere was buried in the Old Granary Burial Ground in the middle of Boston. It was the same cemetery in which his wives and his parents had been buried. You can still see Paul Revere's burial marker in the little cemetery, which is surrounded by the tall buildings of modern Boston. John Hancock and Samuel Adams are buried there too.

"Cool in thought, ardent in action, he was well adapted to form plans, and to carry them into successful execution," wrote the *Boston Intelligencer* in its obituary for Revere.[1]

The New England states did not forget Paul Revere. Some short accounts of his life appeared soon after his death. They described not only his midnight ride but his abilities in organizing his fellow craftsmen to oppose England. He was so well known in New England that some towns named streets for him. Still, Revere was a local hero; few knew of him outside New England.

Then, in 1861, Henry Wadsworth Longfellow published "Paul Revere's Ride" in the *Atlantic* magazine. It began with those famous opening lines:

"Listen my children, and you shall hear,

Of the midnight ride of Paul Revere . . ."[2]

The poem includes some events that never happened: Paul Revere rowing himself across the Charles River, receiving a lantern signal that sent him to Lexington, and reaching both Lexington and Concord on his ride.

Nevertheless, the poem has a driving rhythm and an exciting story line that made it immediately popular. It was published in schoolbooks, and generations of children had to memorize it. Soon Paul Revere was famous all over the United States. Oddly enough, the author of the poem, Henry Wadsworth Longfellow, was the grandson of Peleg Wadsworth. He was the man who had charged Paul Revere with failing to obey orders on the Penobscot Expedition.

Fueled by the poem, interest in Paul Revere kept growing. In 1885, a competition was held to design a statue of him. The winning design showed Revere on horseback. In 1891, the first full-length biography appeared. It was written by Elbridge Henry Goss, who interviewed some people who had actually known Paul Revere. In 1905, a composer published a march called "Paul Revere's Ride."

All this attention to Paul Revere spurred efforts to preserve his home on North Square. By the end of the nineteenth century, this old building had become a run-down tenement occupied by poor families. A grandson of Revere, John P. Reynolds, started a movement to save his ancestor's house. After being restored, the house was opened to the public in 1908. The Paul Revere Memorial Association, which operates the house, supports research on Paul Revere and runs educational programs.

Today visitors to Boston can also see the Old North Church (Christ Church) and Revere's statue, which was erected in a small park near the Revere house. Across the Charles River, in Charlestown, the *Constitution* is now a museum. In nearby Lexington, the Buckman Tavern and the Hancock-Clarke House, Paul Revere's destination in Lexington, are museums too. Every year, on Patriots' Day—April 19—part of Paul Revere's ride

is recreated in Lexington with a rider dressed in eighteenth-century clothing.

Museums, a statue, a holiday, and a poem are not all that remind us of the man who made the midnight ride. Paul Revere was a patriot, but he was also a craftsman and an industrialist. Today most of his silver pieces are in museums. The Museum of Fine Arts in Boston has a large collection of his work, ranging from the famous punch bowl to a variety of teapots. It also has the most famous

*Paul Revere's house on North Square in Boston had three stories when the Revere family lived there. Now it is an historical landmark open to the public.*

portrait of him, painted by John Singleton Copley. Paul Revere's engravings are owned by a number of museums.

Paul Revere's foundry was a prosperous but small business when its founder was alive. By the mid-twentieth century, the firm had merged with others and become Revere Copper and Brass. This firm was dissolved in the 1990s, and two separate firms were created with the Revere name. One is Revere Copper Products, Inc., which makes copper for use in products ranging from electric switches to computer circuit boards. The other is the Revere Ware Corporation, which makes metal kitchenware such as pots and pans.

There was a member of the Revere family working at the firm that became Revere Copper Products until recently. Paul Revere, Jr., a direct descendent of Paul Revere, was sales manager for Revere Copper Products when he retired on January 1, 1996.

Paul Revere's legacy lives on in the nation he helped to create.

# CHRONOLOGY

1734—Born in Boston, colony of Massachusetts, December 21.

1754—Father, Paul Revere, dies July 22.

1756—Ends apprenticeship and becomes silversmith; Joins expedition in French and Indian Wars.

1757—Marries Sarah Orne, August 17.

1758—First child, Deborah, born April 8.

1760—French and Indian Wars end; Joins Freemasons.

1765—Stamp Act passed; Goods seized to pay debt; Joins Sons of Liberty.

1767—Townshend Acts, including tax on tea, passed.

1768—Engraves political cartoons; Britain sends troops to Boston.

1770—Boston Massacre; Buys first house in Boston.

1773—Sarah Revere dies; Marries Rachel Walker, October 10; Boston Tea Party occurs; Rides to New York and Philadelphia.

1774—Intolerable Acts close port of Boston and put Massachusetts under military rule; Rides to First Continental Congress in Philadelphia; Rides to Portsmouth, New Hampshire; Joshua, first child by Rachel, born December 7.

1775—Rides to Lexington April 18–19 to warn patriots British troops are coming; American Revolution begins; Engraves money for Massachusetts to pay troops.

1776—Declaration of Independence signed by Continental Congress; Put in charge of Fort William on Castle Island.

1777—Mother, Deborah Hitchborn Revere, dies May 23.

1778—France becomes an ally of the United States; Joins American-French expedition to Rhode Island.

1779—Dismissed from Castle Island after participating in Penobscot Expedition.

1781—Battle of Yorktown, Virginia ends American Revolution.

1782—Acquitted of charges brought after Penobscot Expedition.

1785—Opens new shop in Boston to sell hardware.

1788—Sets up foundry in North Boston; Works for adoption of new United States Constitution, which becomes law in summer.

1792—Casts first church bell for Cockerel Church.

1800—Buys land for foundry in Canton, Massachusetts, to make first sheet copper in United States.

1803—Revere sheet copper used to cover bottom of the *Constitution*.

1813—Rachel Revere dies June 26.

1818—Dies May 10.

# CHAPTER NOTES

## Chapter 1

1. David Hackett Fischer, *Paul Revere's Ride* (New York: Oxford University Press, 1994), p. 104.

2. Ibid., p. 106.

3. Ibid.

4. Ibid., p. 109.

5. Ibid., p. 110.

6. Ibid., p. 130.

7. Ibid.

8. *Paul Revere's Three Accounts of His Famous Ride* (Boston: Massachusetts Historical Society, 1976), n.p.

9. Fischer, p. 131.

10. *Paul Revere's Three Accounts of His Famous Ride*, n.p.

11. Ibid.

12. Fischer, p. 136.

13. Ibid., p. 136–137.

## Chapter 2

1. Esther Forbes, *Paul Revere and the World He Lived In* (Boston: Houghton Mifflin, 1942), p. 13.

2. Ibid., pp. 182–183.

3. Louis B. Wright, *Life in Colonial America* (New York: G. P. Putnam's Sons, 1965), pp. 136–137.

4. Forbes, p. 29.

5. Janine E. Skerry, "The Revolutionary Revere: A Critical Assessment of the Silver of Paul Revere," in Nina Zannieri, Patrick Leehey, et al., *Paul Revere—Artisan, Businessman and Patriot: The Man Behind the Myth* (Boston: University Publishing Associates, Inc., 1988), p. 46.

## Chapter 3

1. Janine E. Skerry, "The Revolutionary Revere: A Critical Assessment of the Silver of Paul Revere," in Nina Zannieri, Patrick Leehey, et al., *Paul Revere—Artisan, Businessman and Patriot: The Man Behind the Myth* (Boston: University Publishing Associates, Inc., 1988), p. 49.

2. Ibid., p. 47.

3. Esther Forbes, *Paul Revere and the World He Lived In* (Boston: Houghton Mifflin, 1942), p. 61.

4. Ibid., p. 68.

5. *The American Heritage History of the Thirteen Colonies* (American Heritage Publishing Company, 1967), p. 347.

6. Forbes, p. 65.

7. Ibid., pp. 110–112.

8. David Hackett Fischer, *Paul Revere's Ride* (New York: Oxford University Press, 1994), p. 14.

9. Robert Dubuque, "The Painter and the Portrait: John Singleton Copley's Portrait of Paul Revere," *Revere House Gazette*, Autumn 1989, p. 5.

10. Ibid.

## Chapter 4

1. Esther Forbes, *Paul Revere and the World He Lived In* (Boston: Houghton Mifflin, 1942), p. 102.

2. Clarence S. Brigham American Antiquarian Society, *Paul Revere's Engravings* (New York: Atheneum, 1969), p. 43.

3. Forbes, p. 137.

4. *The American Heritage History of the Thirteen Colonies* (American Heritage Publishing Company, 1967), p. 347.

5. Brigham, Plate 22.

6. Elbridge Henry Goss, *The Life Of Colonel Paul Revere* (Boston: Cupples, 1891), vol. II, p. 440.

7. Ibid.

8. Forbes, p. 155.

9. Museum of Fine Arts, Boston, *Paul Revere's Boston, 1735–1818* (Museum of Fine Arts, Boston, 1975), p. 112.

## Chapter 5

1. Esther Forbes, *Paul Revere and the World He Lived In* (Boston: Houghton Mifflin, 1942), p. 181.

2. Elbridge Henry Goss, *The Life of Colonel Paul Revere* (Boston: Cupples, 1891), vol. I, p. 110.

3. Henry Steele Commager and Richard B. Morris, eds., *The Spirit of 'Seventy-Six* (New York: Bobbs Merrill Co., Inc., 1958), vol. I, p. 5.

4. David Hackett Fischer, *Paul Revere's Ride* (New York: Oxford University Press, 1994), pp. 25–26.

5. Forbes, p. 208.

6. Roger N. Parks, *Roads and Travel in New England, 1790–1840* (Sturbridge, Mass.: Old Sturbridge Village, 1967), pp. 7–8.

7. R. Ernest Dupuy and Trevor N. Dupuy, *The Compact History of the Revolutionary War* (New York: Hawthorne Books, 1963), p. 27.

8. Fischer, p. 87.

9. Ibid., pp. 87–88.

10. Ibid., p. 99.

11. Ibid., p. 100.

12. Ibid., p. 97.

## Chapter 6

1. R. Ernest Dupuy and Trevor N. Dupuy, *The Compact History of the Revolutionary War* (New York: Hawthorne Books, 1963), p. 37.

2. Esther Forbes, *Paul Revere and the World He Lived In* (Boston: Houghton Mifflin, 1942), pp. 283–284.

3. Ibid.

4. Ibid.

5. Ibid.

6. Ibid.

7. Dupuy and Dupuy, p. 53.

## Chapter 7

1. David Hackett Fischer, *Paul Revere's Ride* (New York: Oxford University Press, 1994), p. 291.

2. Declaration of Independence, July 4, 1776.

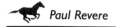 

3. Elbridge Henry Goss, *The Life of Colonel Paul Revere* (Boston: Cupples, 1891), vol. I, p. 300.

4. Esther Forbes, *Paul Revere and the World He Lived In* (Boston: Houghton Mifflin, 1942), p. 339.

5. Goss, vol. I, pp. 305–307.

6. Ibid., vol. II, p. 364.

7. Jon M. Nielson, *"Penobscot: From the Jaws of Victory—Our Navy's Worse Defeat,"* American Neptune, vol. 37, no. 4, October 1977, p. 300.

8. Goss, vol. II, p. 375.

9. Ibid., p. 376.

10. Forbes, p. 359.

11. Goss, vol. II, pp. 337–338.

12. L. F. Willard, "Students for the Defense," *Yankee Magazine*, September 1972, p. 123.

## Chapter 8

1. Elbridge Henry Goss, *The Life of Colonel Paul Revere* (Boston: Cupples, 1891), vol. II, p. 383.

2. Ibid., p. 512.

3. Ibid., p. 516.

4. Deborah A. Federhen, "From Artisan to Entrepreneur; Paul Revere's Silver Shop Operation," in Nina Zannieri, Patrick Leehey, et al., *Paul Revere—Artisan, Businessman and Patriot: The Man Behind the Myth* (Boston: University Publishing Associates, Inc., 1988), p. 83.

5. Goss, vol. II, p. 531.

6. Ibid., p. 454.

## Chapter 9

1. Esther Forbes, *Paul Revere and the World He Lived In* (Boston: Houghton Mifflin, 1942), p. 387.

2. Elbridge Henry Goss, *The Life of Colonel Paul Revere* (Boston: Cupples, 1891), vol. II, pp. 554–555.

3. Ibid., p. 544.

4. Ibid., p. 611.

5. Museum of Fine Arts, Boston, *Paul Revere's Boston*, 1735–1818 (Boston: Museum of Fine Arts, Boston, 1975), p. 210.

6. Goss, p. 561.

7. Forbes, p. 427.

8. *Paul Revere's Boston*, 1735–1818, p. 210.

## Chapter 10

1. Patrick M. Leehey, "Reconstructing Paul Revere: An Overview of His Ancestry, Life and Work," in Nina Zannieri, Patrick Leehey, et. al., *Paul Revere—Artisan, Businessman and Patriot*: The Man Behind the Myth (Boston: University Publishing Associates, Inc., 1988), p. 33.

2. Longfellow, Henry Wadsworth, *Paul Revere's Ride* (New York: Dutton Children's Books, 1990).

# GLOSSARY

**activist**—A person who uses strong actions to achieve goals.

**ambush**—A trap in which people conceal themselves so they can attack by surprise.

**barnacles**—Shelled sea animals that affix themselves to surfaces such as a ship or dock.

**breeches**—Short trousers that fit tightly just below the knee.

**commemorate**—To be a memorial for a person or event.

**engraving**—Figures and letters cut into a surface for printing.

**exile**—Removal from one's native country by force.

**expedition**—A journey for a special purpose.

**flagship**—The ship in a fleet that carries the commander and flies his flag.

**fortified**—Made safe by grouping artillery such as cannons.

**foundry**—An establishment where metal is cast.

**gauntlet**—Two lines of armed men who strike a victim who runs between the lines.

**labor intensive**—Using a high number of workers.

**monopoly**—Exclusive power to buy or sell some product or service.

**musket**—A shoulder gun carried by infantry.

**parliament**—The highest law-making body in a nation or state.

**peal**—The loud ringing of bells.

**punch bowl**—A large bowl from which beverages are served.

**sideboard**—A piece of dining room furniture that holds plates and utensils for eating.

**taunted**—Challenged in an insulting way.

**transport ships**—Unarmed ships that carry goods or people.

**volley**—The firing of a number of missiles at the same time.

# FURTHER READING

Athearn, Robert G. *American Heritage Illustrated History of the United States*. vols. II, III, IV. Parsippany, NJ: Silver Burdett Press, Inc., 1989.

Barker, John. *The British in Boston. Being the Diary of Lieutenant John Barker of the King's Own Regiment From November 15, 1774 to May 31, 1776*. Cambridge: Harvard University Press, 1924.

Earle, Alice Morse. *Home Life in Colonial Days*. Middle Village, New York: Jonathan David Publishers, Inc., 1975.

Fischer, David Hackett. *Paul Revere's Ride*. New York: Oxford University Press, 1994.

Fischer, Leonard Everett. *The Silversmiths*. New York: Franklin Watts, 1964.

Folmsbee, Beulah. *A Little History of the Horn Book*. Boston: The Horn Book, Inc., 1942.

Forbes, Esther. *Johnny Tremain*. Boston: Houghton Mifflin, 1943. (Newbery-winning young adult novel about a teenager in mid-1770s Boston who becomes a messenger like Paul Revere. Revere and other historical characters appear in book.)

———. *Paul Revere and the World He Lived In*. Boston: Houghton Mifflin, 1942.

Longfellow, Henry Wadsworth. *Paul Revere's Ride*. New York: Dutton Children's Books, 1990.

# INDEX

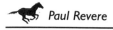